Paddling Colorado

HELP US KEEP THIS GUIDE UP TO DATE

Every effort has been made by the author and editors to make this guide as accurate and useful as possible. However, many things can change after a guide is published—trails are rerouted, regulations change, techniques evolve, facilities come under new management, etc.

We welcome your comments concerning your experiences with this guide and how you feel it could be improved and kept up to date. While we may not be able to respond to all comments and suggestions, we'll take them to heart, and we'll also make certain to share them with the author. Please send your comments and suggestions to the following address:

The Globe Pequot Press
Reader Response/Editorial Department
P.O. Box 480
Guilford, CT 06437

Or you may e-mail us at: editorial@GlobePequot.com

Thanks for your input, and happy travels!

Paddling Colorado

A Guide to the State's Best Paddling Routes

Dunbar Hardy

GUILFORD, CONNECTICUT
HELENA, MONTANA
AN IMPRINT OF THE GLOBE PEQUOT PRESS

To buy books in quantity for corporate use
or incentives, call **(800) 962-0973**
or e-mail **premiums@GlobePequot.com.**

FALCONGUIDES®

Project manager: David Legere
Text designer: Nancy Freeborn
Layout artist: Kim Burdick
Maps © Morris Book Publishing, LLC
All photos by Dunbar Hardy unless indicated otherwise.

Library of Congress Cataloging-in-Publication Data is
available on file.

ISBN 978-0-7627-4520-3

Printed in the United States of America

10 9 8 7 6 5 4 3 2 1

To my mother and father, Mary and Robyn, who put me in my first canoe before I can even remember. I thank you both for helping me to grow up on the water and to forever appreciate its beauty.

Also Kells Hogan, who introduced me to my first whitewater river. He first showed me the world of moving water, and my life has been forever changed.

And Brennan Guth, who was lost to the river. I shared many days on the water with him, and his passing taught me about the water's power.

The beautiful San Juan Mountains rise in southern Colorado.

Contents

Flatwater Tours—Lakes and Reservoirs (North–South)

Map Legend

Transportation

- Freeway/Interstate Highway (70)
- U.S. Highway (50)
- State Highway (13)
- Other Road
- Railroad

Water Features

- Body of Water
- Major River
- Minor River or Creek
- Intermittent River or Creek

Symbols

- Boat Launch
- Bridge
- Building/Point of Interest
- Campground
- Put-In/Takeout

Land Management

- National Park/Forest
- State Park, Wilderness Area

N — True North (Magnetic North is approximately 11.0° East)

Wyoming

Colorado

11

DINOSAUR
NATIONAL
MONUMENT

318

13

Craig

10

Yampa R.

40

Steamboat
Springs

130

70

230

230

North Platte R.

125

127

1

14

125

Laramie R.

Longs P
14,255

40

131

134

Granby

34

31

ROCKY MOUNTAIN
NATIONAL PARK

14

9

40

12

Rangely

White R.

64

Meeker

139

13

131

15

Eagle

Vail

Silverthorne

6

40

70

13

Rifle

Colorado R.

Glenwood Springs

24

91

9

285

13

Carbondale

16

82

9

17

Aspen

Leadville

70

Grand
Junction

Fruita

65

133

▲ Mt. Elbert
14,433 ft.

24

9

COLORADO
NATIONAL
MONUMENT

50

Gunnison R.

92

BLACK CANYON OF
THE GUNNISON
NATIONAL MONUMENT

18

CONTINENTAL DIVIDE

Buena
Vista

19

Delta

Colorado
Utah

141

90

23

21

145

62

22

50

92

33

Gunnison

*Blue Mesa
Reservoir*

20

Montrose

50

285

Salida

50

141

114

17

149

GREAT SAND DUNES
NATIONAL PARK

491

145

550

8

285

Monte Vista

160

Alamo

Cortez

160

34

25

Pagosa Springs

160

26

Durango

84

142

MESA VERDE
NATIONAL PARK

160

151

24

17

9

491

550

Aztec

64

84

285

64

Farmington

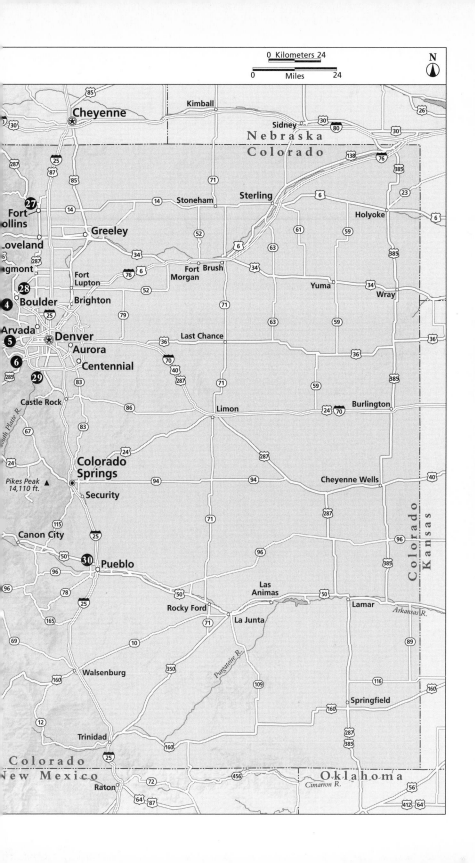

Acknowledgments

First off, I would like to thank all those people who pulled over to offer me a ride as I stood next to the road shivering. I've sat by many rivers waiting for rides, and this is a huge thanks to those brave souls who let this stinky, wet, and cold paddler crawl into their car for a ride back up to the put-in. I would also like to say thank you to the Colorado Environmental Coalition and American Whitewater for dedicated and persistent advocacy work in protecting Colorado's paddling resources.

Another round of thanks goes to those individuals who offered their support and encouragement of this project. These people contributed their experience and even photographs to help make this a more thorough guidebook—Landis Arnold, Wildwasser Sport; Kent Ford, Performance Video; Max Young, Renaissance Guides; Marty Genereux, Centennial Canoes; Earl Richmond and Heather Gorby, Colorado Kayak Supply; Nathan Fey, American Whitewater; Eric Bader, Boulder Outdoor Center; CJ Harrington, Pagosa Outside; Bryan Kelsen Photography; William Luster Photography; and Eugene Buchanan, *Paddling Life* magazine.

Last but not least is a huge debt of gratitude to my paddling partners who have been patient with me as I asked them to wait a second while I scrambled to take photos or motivate them to paddle when perhaps they really didn't want to: my incredibly patient wife, Julia Wieck; the entire Scarpella family—Brian, Allison, Toby, and Finn; Chad and Stephanie Crabtree; Taylor Beavers; Brad and Megan Higinbotham; Katie Selby; Christie Dobson; Woody Calloway; Jim and Ruth Olson; and Andrew Wracher.

Introduction

Welcome to Colorado—home of the Rocky Mountains. Known for its numerous snow-covered mountains and dramatic scenery, Colorado has been characterized as a skier's paradise and a home for those who love snow. This may be true for part of the year, but come warmer weather and melting snow, Colorado makes an abrupt transition into being a home for paddlers. These same snow-covered peaks become a stunning backdrop to spring and summertime paddling options all over the state, with many options extending into the fall. With 300-plus days of sunshine a year and fresh clean air, Colorado is a prime paddling destination for those who relish the outdoors and welcome the beauty of clean rivers, pristine lakes, a great climate, and beautiful scenery.

Another great thing about paddling in Colorado is the number of options that exist for paddlers of all skill levels. Countless mountain lakes and reservoirs offer flatwater enthusiasts still-water paddling with mountain views in every direction. Beginning paddlers will find abundant sections appropriate for learning on almost every river in the state. Intermediate paddlers will be thrilled with the numerous quality sections available to them, while advanced/expert paddlers will be challenged to tackle some of the most difficulty whitewater found anywhere. Whether a flatwater paddler, a Class I beginner, a Class III intermediate, or a Class V expert, Colorado has classic paddling for everyone.

Lay of the Land

Believe it or not, not all Colorado is full of mountains. The eastern side of the state is a sloping high plain of open expanse that extends toward the flatlands of Nebraska, Kansas, and Oklahoma. This part of the state is better known for its agriculture than its paddling. Bumping up against the mountains is an area known as the Front Range, which is home to most of the state's population and the cities of Pueblo, Colorado Springs, Denver, Boulder, and Fort Collins. There are paddling opportunities along the Front Range, as well as crowds. Heading farther west, up and over the Continental Divide, is the central part of the state and its highest mountains. This is home to the majority of ski areas, as well as abundant snowmelt paddling options. Heading even farther west is the part of the state known as the Western Slope. The mountain scenery eventually transitions to a dry high desert–like environment as Colorado gives way to the sandstone cliffs of Utah.

With such a variety of ecosystems and scenery throughout the geography of the state, the different paddling options are equally varied. Included in this guidebook are runs set in the incredibly urban setting of downtown Denver to runs on the remote lower canyons of the Dolores River tucked away down in the southwest corner of the state. Offering whatever style of paddling you most enjoy coupled with a variety of settings and beautiful scenery, Colorado affords a lifetime of diverse paddling options.

Safety on the Water

Do your homework before setting out for a paddle: Check the weather forecast, check the water levels, have the proper gear and equipment, have at least one paddling partner, and have a clear plan with an estimated take-out time and location. These simple rules are very important and must be practiced every time you go out for a paddle in order to prevent potential accidents and be prepared for any accidents that do happen.

Be prepared for the weather: Know what is forecast for the day of your paddle, as well as the days ahead if launching on a multiday paddle.

Water Levels: Check the water level of your intended run before putting in, and be sure the current level is within the recommended flow range. (See the appendix for specific contact information.)

Bring proper clothing and equipment: Always wear a properly fitted personal flotation device (PFD), and wear appropriate clothing layers to stay warm in wet and cold. At least one first-aid kit is recommended within each group.

Paddle with partners: There is safety, and enjoyment, in numbers; do your best to never paddle alone.

Let others know your plan: Relay the day's paddling plan to others outside the paddling group who will know when and where to look for you if you don't arrive when expected.

Be prepared: Prepare for the worst by taking extra clothing, bringing a first-aid kit, and having first-aid/river-rescue training.

Know your capabilities: Be honest about your skill level, and always paddle within your abilities.

Understand difficulty ratings: Many rivers increase in difficulty with an increase in flow, so know what you are getting into before you actually enter the water. Following are the general classifications of river difficulty:

- **Class I: Easy.** Flatwater or moving water with easy, small waves, if any; little to no maneuvering; no obstructions.

- **Class II: Medium.** Easy rapids with a few small obstructions that are easily avoidable; increased water speed; clear routes downstream.

- **Class III: Difficult.** Numerous rapids with larger irregular waves requiring more precise maneuvering between obstacles; increased water speed. More-obstructed routes may require scouting.

- **Class IV: Very Difficult.** Longer more powerful rapids with large waves between large rocks and other obstacles; very obstructed route. High skill level with scouting is highly recommended.

- **Class V: Extremely Difficult.** Long, violent rapids that drop steeply with extremely fast current; complex route-finding required between potentially hazardous features. Extensive experience and skill recommended; scouting is mandatory.

- **Class VI: Unrunnable.**

Flows

Each river run outlined in this guide has a recommended flow range coupled with the river difficulty rating. Of course sections of rivers can be paddled outside the recommended flow range, but you risk a paddle of less quality if the waters are too low or one that's more difficult—and dangerous—if the waters are higher than the recommended flow.

In order to stay within a section of river that matches your difficulty level, check the flow of the section as close as possible to the time and day you are planning to paddle. Use the water level resources provided in the appendix of this guide to check the most current flows. Then reference the current flow with the recommended flow range for the section you are planning to paddle. This will give you an informed idea as to what to expect regarding the character and difficulty of that section prior to putting in. Doing your homework before paddling is an important part of ensuring a safe and enjoyable day on the water.

With a few exceptions, there is a distinct season to most of the paddling within Colorado. Generally speaking, Colorado's rivers tend to run off and swell with melting snows in late spring (April and May), peak in early summer (May and June), and drop to low flows by late summer and fall (July through September).

Some of the rivers outlined in this guide are dam controlled and thus no longer follow this natural seasonal flow. It is important to verify the actual dam releases and flows of these rivers if you intend to paddle them. The operations of these dams will ultimately determine the true length, or season, of the river's run, as well as the true flow range from low to high water.

How to Use This Guide

Each paddle description begins with a section that provides nuts-and-bolts information on that specific paddling destination. Each of these at-a-glance items is described below:

Section map: A general map is included with each river description to help paddlers get oriented in finding the access points for the put-in and takeout. This map also shows a few of the larger characteristics of the section to be paddled.

General description: This briefly outlines the waterway's geographic location, outlines its general characteristics and paddling quality, and highlights the overall route.

Section description: More specific information on the characteristics and qualities of a specific section to be paddled.

Distance: A fairly accurate measurement of the section to be paddled, measured in miles.

Difficulty: The ideal skill level recommended for the section to be paddled.

Craft: The recommended type of watercraft for the section to be paddled. (*Note:* Inflatable kayaks and canoes are included in the "recreation boat type" category, which distinguishes the run as having more flatwater than whitewater.)

Approximate paddling time: A range of time, measured in hours, required to paddle the section at the fastest speed as well as at a slower, more leisurely pace.

Flows: The recommended flow range, measured in cubic feet per second (cfs), that will maintain the highest quality paddling while keeping this section within its previously mentioned difficulty rating. When applicable, dam–controlled sections are noted, providing paddlers with a heads-up that dam operations will ultimately determine the flows.

Season: A recommended time frame for the best paddling flows on the section to be paddled. When applicable, dam-controlled sections are noted, providing paddlers with a heads-up that dam operations will ultimately determine the season.

Put-in: A recommended launching access point to begin the described section for paddling.

Takeout: A recommended exit access point to conclude the described section for paddling.

Shuttle: Detailed route descriptions for driving and completing the shuttle to access both the put-in and takeout for the described paddle.

In addition: Additional paddling options related to the described paddle. This may include a higher or lower access point to lengthen or shorten the run or a brief description of a more-advanced nearby paddling route that's beyond the scope of this guide.

4

The routes in the Flatwater Tours chapter include information on launch sites and access points rather than put-in, takeout, and shuttle descriptions. These write-ups also include sources of information on the specific reservoirs and lakes and related parklands plus "honorable mentions" for additional paddling options in the area.

Giving Back

What makes Colorado so special is its natural resources. Rivers and lakes are definitely included in that list of resources. The numerous free-flowing rivers and creeks that gush out of the mountains are gifts to be respected and cherished. The dedicated care and commitment of people and organizations have kept the majority of these paddling resources available for future generations to enjoy. If not for these groups and other people who love Colorado, we might not have the many options for paddling that exist today for all of us.

Whether you're visiting and paddling in Colorado for the first time or putting in for another day on the local run, please consider becoming involved in river and wilderness conservation within the state. The future protection of our resources depends on community involvement. For additional information on statewide and national organizations that are actively participating in protecting Colorado's natural resources, see this guide's appendix.

Thank you for your consideration and care for the future of paddling in Colorado.

Front Range
Paddles
(North-South)

1 North Platte River

Tucked up in the northern portion of the state, the North Platte River is formed by the confluence of various streams that drain the Rabbit Ears Wilderness Area to the west and the Medicine Bow Mountains to the east. Coming together in a broad, wide-open valley in the northern portion of the state, the North Platte slides out of the valley and into the Platte River Wilderness Area once it crosses into Wyoming.

Free flowing up here along the border, the North Platte surges with spring snowmelt and runoff, offering some fine remote beginner/intermediate sections of paddling. The North Platte keeps running northward toward the middle of Wyoming. It then makes a hard turn to the east and flows out of the state and into Nebraska, where it runs the length of the state before eventually joining the Missouri River.

Upper Valley

This meandering section of the North Platte is a flat section of river set in a wide valley. If you're looking for a beginner paddle while in the neighborhood, this top section of the North Platte could be an option. Private property lines both sides of the river, so please be respectful of all landowners' requests for privacy.

Distance: 6.0 miles
Difficulty: Class I (beginner)
Craft: Canoes, kayaks, rafts
Approximate paddling time: 3 to 4 hours
Flows: 500 to 1,500 cfs
Season: May through July
Put-in: County Road 6 bridge
Takeout: Routt launch site
Shuttle: To reach the put-in from Walden, head north on Highway 125, turn left (west) onto CR 6 in Cowdrey. Cross the bridge on CR 6—this is the put-in.

To reach the takeout, return to Highway 125 and turn left (north), stay on Highway 125 as it winds around and crosses over the river. Shortly after this bridge, look for signs for Routt launch site. Turn right (east) and follow the signs to the boat launch area—this is the takeout.

Northgate Canyon

Straddling the Colorado-Wyoming border, Northgate Canyon offers some fine intermediate wilderness paddling set in a remote and isolated canyon that flows through the heart of the Platte River Wilderness Area. Rugged slopes, lush forests of firs, and an "out there" feeling all capture the attention of paddlers as they slide downstream from the put-in. A bit of a warm-up is granted before the heart of the whitewater comes in a 4.0-mile section. In the heart of the run, challenging whitewater demands intermediate paddlers' full attention and skill. Paddlers will face Cowpie (Class III+), Narrow Falls (Class III+), Tootsie Roll (Class III), and Stovepipe Rapids (Class III). Just below Stovepipe, a steep 200-yard-long trail climbs up to the takeout.

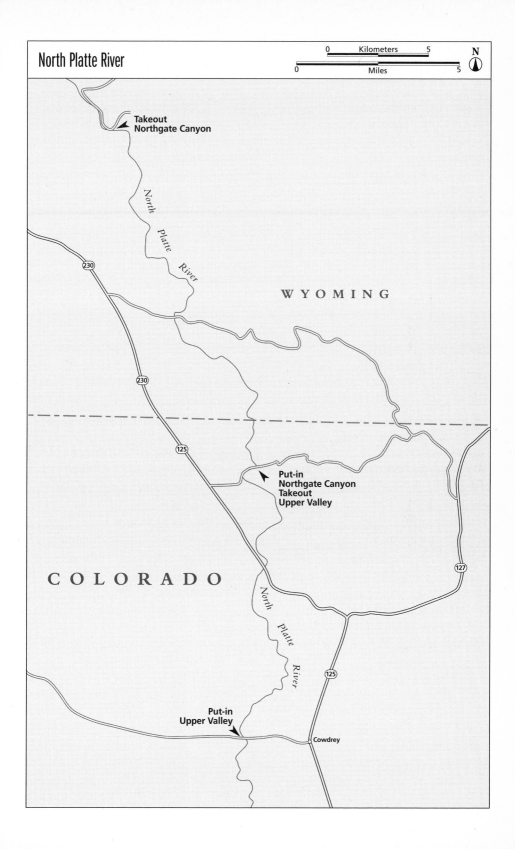

North Platte River

0 Kilometers 5
0 Miles 5

N

Takeout
Northgate Canyon

North Platte River

230

230

125

WYOMING

Put-in
Northgate Canyon
Takeout
Upper Valley

127

COLORADO

North Platte River

125

Put-in
Upper Valley

Cowdrey

Distance: 10.0 miles (longer runs possible)
Difficulty: Class III (intermediate)
Craft: Canoes, kayaks, rafts
Approximate paddling time: 3 to 4 hours
Flows: 500 to 1,500 cfs
Season: May through July
Put-in: Routt launch site
Takeout: Six-Mile Gap (Wyoming)
Shuttle: To reach the put-in from Walden, head north on Highway 125. Passing through Cowdrey, stay on Highway 125 as it winds around and crosses the river. Shortly after this bridge, look for signs for Routt launch site. Turn right (east) and follow the signs to the boat launch area—this is the put-in.

To reach the takeout, return to Highway 125 and turn right (north). Cross into Wyoming, where Colorado Highway 125 becomes Wyoming Highway 230. Four miles north of the border, turn right (east) onto County Road 492 and follow it for 2 miles to a campground and trailhead; this is the takeout.

Additional information: It is possible to continue downstream from the takeout for an additional 7.0 miles of Class II paddling to the Pickaroon Campground takeout, located farther north on Wyoming Highway 230.

2 Poudre River

The Cache la Poudre River tumbles out of the east side of the Medicine Bow Mountains and drains the northern side of Rocky Mountain National Park. As the Poudre gathers its tributaries during late-spring runoff, it runs strong and continuous as it tumbles downstream through a dramatic river canyon. The Poudre River Canyon, a designated Wild and Scenic River corridor, offers beautiful driving along Highway 14, which closely parallels the river throughout the length of the canyon. The river here also offers fine beginner to expert levels of paddling options.

As the Poudre tumbles through its canyon, various sections of the river challenge all skill levels of paddlers. Even beginners will find a quality section worthy of paddling. As the Poudre exits its canyon just west of Fort Collins, various irrigation diversions take water out of its channel. The river flattens out as it heads east onto the Front Range plains toward Greeley, where it eventually becomes another tributary to the South Platte River.

Kinikinik Section

This higher section on the Poudre offers intermediate paddlers their first section of the river. The river is cold, fast, and continuous up here and boogies through endless small waves and riffles. The Class II rapids require no dramatic moves. Swift fastwater set beneath heavily forested mountain hillsides describes the canyon scenery on this section of the river.

Poudre River

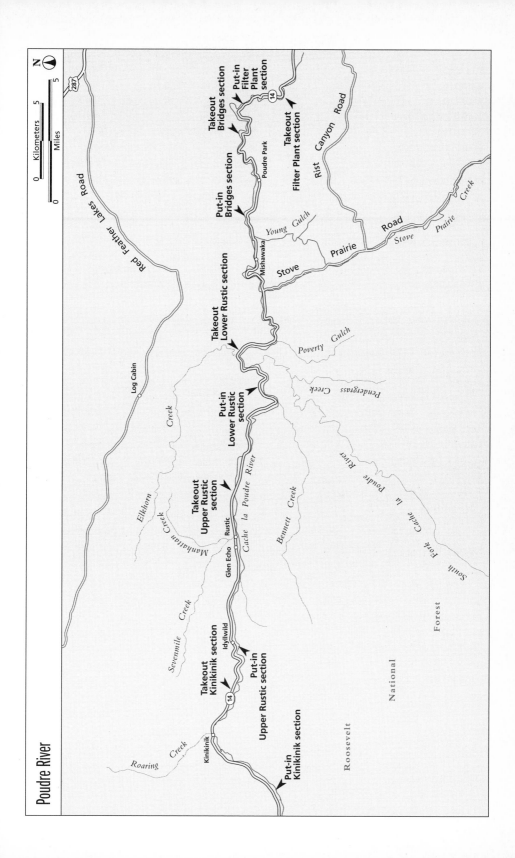

Distance: 6.5 miles
Difficulty: Class II (advanced beginner/intermediate)
Craft: Kayaks, canoes
Approximate paddling time: 2 to 3 hours
Flows: 350 to 650 cfs
Season: May through July
Put-in: Sleeping Elephant Campground
Takeout: Pullout just below the fish hatchery

Shuttle: Use Highway 14, which closely parallels the river, as the primary route for access along this section. Both the put-in and takeout are well marked and easy to find.
Additional information: Shortly below the takeout for this section is a series of Class IV rapids called the Miracle Mile, for advanced paddlers. Just upstream of this section is the expert-only Spencer Heights section (Class V).

Upper Rustic Section

This upstream run of the Poudre offers a great intermediate section of enjoyable Class III whitewater set in a little wider river valley. This section offers a shallow roller-coaster ride through an endless number of fun, splashy waves. The rapids fall into the Class III realm, but they are really straightforward—long, choppy rapids, with little technical maneuvering to worry about.

Distance: 7.8 miles (shorter runs possible)
Difficulty: Class III (intermediate)
Craft: Canoes, kayaks, rafts
Approximate paddling time: 2 to 3 hours
Flows: 175 to 600 cfs
Season: May through July
Put-in: Idyllwild
Takeout: Indian Meadows, low highway bridge (Mile Marker 93)

Shuttle: Use Highway 14, which closely parallels the river, as the primary route for access along this section. Both the put-in and takeout are well marked and easy to find.
Additional information: Shortly below the takeout for this section, the Poudre drops into a section known as Grandpa's Gorge (Class IV), for more advanced paddlers.

Lower Rustic Section

This short piece of the Poudre offers a short but sweet intermediate section of enjoyable Class III whitewater similar to the Upper Rustic waters previously described. Squeezed between harder rapids upstream and nearly unrunnable whitewater below, the Lower Rustic is a nearly continuous section of straightforward waves with little obstacles to maneuver around. Buckle up and charge through some fun waves. Highway 14, which closely parallels the river, makes the shuttle for this paddle super easy and worth a possible repeat run.

A group of kayakers charges the correct line down ▶
Pineview Falls.

Distance: 3.0 miles
Difficulty: Class II–III (intermediate)
Craft: Canoes, kayaks, rafts
Approximate paddling time: 1 to 2 hours
Flows: 175 to 600 cfs
Season: May through July
Put-in: Mountain Park Campground
Takeout: Narrows Campground
Shuttle: Use Highway 14, which closely parallels the river, as the primary route for access along this section. Both the put-in and takeout are well marked and easy to find.
Additional information: Just above the put-in for this section is a series of Class IV rapids, located just below Bennett Creek, for the more advanced paddler. Just below the takeout, the Poudre drops into a 3.0-mile expert-only section, aptly called the Narrows (Class V).

Bridges Section

This section of the Poudre offers up a fine, easy intermediate run. Fun, busy water carries paddlers through the roadside river canyon, where they have to navigate two tricky bridges and a rapid just upstream of the first bridge. Exercise caution with these hazards. The rest of this fine, short run is a good bet for the after-work crowd.

Distance: 2.0 miles
Difficulty: Class II–III (intermediate)
Craft: Canoes, kayaks, rafts
Approximate paddling time: 1 to 2 hours
Flows: 200 to 600 cfs
Season: May through July
Put-in: Pullout just below Pine View Falls (Mile Marker 112.7)
Takeout: Pullout just above diversion dam (Mile Marker 114.7)
Shuttle: Use Highway 14, which closely parallels the river, as the primary access route along this section.
Additional information: Just above the put-in for this run, 8.0 miles of Class III–IV whitewater, known as the Mishawaka Run, will challenge more advanced paddlers. Use a put-in near Stevens Campground.

Filter Plant Section

This is the classic beginner section of the Lower Poudre. Still set in the canyon, as craggy rocks tower above the river, the filter plant run sees all types of paddlers and tubers. In part because of its proximity to Fort Collins, it's popular as an after-work run. The river channel is pretty wide-open, with straightforward series of waves and smaller rapids. The big one on the run is Mad Dog Rapid (Class II+–III-), located on a hard right turn. The rest of this run is good-to-go for anyone.

Distance: 2.5 miles

Difficulty: Class II–III- (beginner/intermediate)

Craft: Canoes, kayaks, rafts

Approximate paddling time: 1 to 2 hours

Flows: 200 to 1,000 cfs

Season: May through July

Put-in: Below the filter plant (near Mile Marker 116.8)

Takeout: Picnic Rock River Access (Mile Marker 119)

Shuttle: Use Highway 14, which closely parallels the river, as the primary route for access along this section. The takeout is well marked—look for signs indicating PICNIC ROCK RIVER ACCESS. Pay the use fee for this access, and make sure you don't miss the takeout—a diversion dam lies just downstream.

To reach the put-in, head upstream (west) on Highway 14 for 3 miles to Mile Marker 116.8, which is below the actual turnoff for the filter plant. Unload next to the river, and park in the designated parking area across the highway—this is the put-in.

3 St. Vrain River

The St. Vrain drainage begins high up on the flanks of 13,000-plus-foot mountains in the Indian Peaks Wilderness Area, which drains the east side of Rocky Mountain National Park. Falling downhill in various forks, the main stem of the St. Vrain River doesn't completely come together until the quaint foothills town of Lyons.

Upstream of here, the North Fork plummets through a relatively unknown river canyon of granite boulders before finally easing down in its last few miles above town, offering some fine beginner and intermediate paddling. The South Fork drops down a rugged river canyon that proves to be expert-only terrain.

Because of its relatively small drainage and split flow, the window for paddling on the St. Vrain is relatively short and is a technical shallow-paddling affair at best. If the water is there and you are in the area, check out paddling on the lower sections of the river and enjoy some surfing in the park in town.

Lower North Fork Section

This short section of the Lower North Fork offers a fine, busy intermediate piece of paddling. An easy shuttle will get you on the water quickly, enjoying quick boogie moves around small rocks and scraping over others. When the flow is good, you'll find a steady current. Paddlers will focus on frequent smaller rapids, not really noticing the nearby road that closely parallels the river. This section is also used as a bit higher put-in for the slightly easier Apple Valley section downstream.

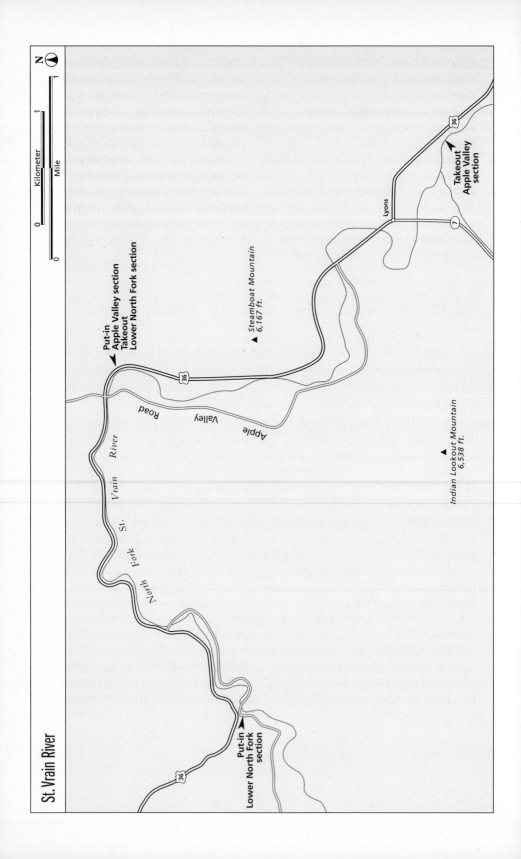

St. Vrain River

Distance: 2.5 miles
Difficulty: Class II+–III (intermediate)
Craft: Kayaks
Approximate paddling time: 1 hour
Flows: 150 to 400 cfs
Season: May through June
Put-in: County Road 80 bridge
Takeout: Apple Valley Bridge
Shuttle: From downtown Lyons head north on U.S. Highway 36 a few miles to Apple Valley Road. Turn left (south) and cross the bridge; park in the river access lot just upstream on the right side of the river—this is the takeout.

To reach the put-in, continue heading upstream (north) on US 36, look for CR 80 and turn left (west). Head upstream as the road closely parallels the river and look for a bridge over the river; this is the put-in.

Roads along this entire stretch of river make it possible to scout while driving the shuttle to see exactly what you are getting into.

Additional information: A 2.5-mile expert-only (Class IV–V) section lies just upstream of this run. Use the trailhead put-in below Button Rock Reservoir.

Apple Valley Section

This bottom section of the North Fork of the St. Vrain offers a slightly easier piece of paddling than the previous upstream run. The Apple Valley run is a nice advanced-beginner run through a pleasant rural valley away from the busy tourist-laden highway. Set in a more open valley with distant red sandstone cliffs, the river channel snakes and wanders over shallow rocks and passes underneath low branches. The last portion of this runs almost doubles in flow as the North and South Forks of the St. Vrain join together in the middle of Lyons. Cruise through town, and take out at the man-made surfing spots in Lyons Park.

Distance: 4.0 miles
Difficulty: Class II–III- (advanced beginner/intermediate)
Craft: Kayaks
Approximate paddling time: 1 to 2 hours
Flows: 150 to 400 cfs
Season: May through June
Put-in: Apple Valley Bridge
Takeout: Lyons Park
Shuttle: From downtown Lyons, head north on US 36 a few miles to Apple Valley Road. Turn left (south) and cross the bridge. Park in the river access lot just upstream on the right side of the river; this is the put-in.

To reach the takeout, return to Lyons on US 36. Turn left (east) at the traffic light upon entering town. Look for Lyons Park on the right-hand (south) side of US 36 on the east edge of town near the Black Bear Inn—this is the takeout.

Additional information: For those budding playboaters seeking to work on their surfing skills, be sure to spend some time at the man-made features in the park at the takeout. There is expert-only technical paddling available on the Narrows section of the South Fork (Class V). Check it out by heading up Highway 7 near Mile Marker 29.

Lower North Fork of the St. Vrain River.

4 Boulder Creek

This is a relatively small drainage for runoff, but because of the outdoor-oriented nature of the community of Boulder, Boulder Creek gets paddled frequently. It literally flows out of the mountains and directly through town.

Draining the Indian Peaks Wilderness Area above Eldora Ski Area, Boulder Creek tumbles through the congested and dramatic scenery of Boulder Canyon. Perhaps better for rock climbing than paddling, Boulder Canyon does offer a short window of incredibly technical, expert-only paddling.

As the creek tumbles out of the canyon on the west side of Boulder, it courses through a section of man-made rapids and surf ledges. The small creek charges through town and eases as it continues heading east onto the plains. Eventually Boulder Creek enters the St. Vrain River, which then flows into the South Platte River.

Town Run

A small window of good water for paddling is the hardest part of this run. Once the water is here, a paddle through the heart of Boulder makes for a fun and thrilling urban-creeking experience for intermediate paddlers. Because of its narrow channel, overhanging tree branches in places, and numerous shallow rocks, this is not the nicest beginner zone, even though the actual rapids are not that difficult.

Put in on the west side of town, and begin with some nearly continuous small ledges and rocky rapids. When the water is high, it is a nearly nonstop rocket ride. At more reasonable water levels, smaller eddies can be found below some drops. Numerous river modifications have been made to make certain ledges and small diversions more paddling-friendly. The whitewater calms down a bit throughout the length of the run as it heads east.

Distance: 2.0 miles
Difficulty: Class II-III (intermediate)
Craft: Kayaks
Approximate paddling time: 1 to 2 hours
Flows: 150 to 400 cfs
Season: May through June
Put-in: Eben G. Fine Park
Takeout: Scott Carpenter Park on 30th Street
Shuttle: To reach the put-in, head west on Arapahoe Avenue off Broadway (the main north-south route through town). At the very western end of Arapahoe Avenue (after Third Street) is Eben G. Fine Park—this is the put-in.

To reach the takeout, head east on Arapahoe to 30th Street. Turn right (south) onto 30th Street, and make an immediate right (west) into Scott Carpenter Park. Head to a parking area near the creek—this is the takeout.

Additional information: It is possible to continue this run all the way out to 55th Street—there are more Class II rapids located downstream of this takeout. Playboaters seeking to work on their skills can head just upstream of the put-in and try surfing some of the numerous man-made play features. Advanced/expert (Class IV-V) runs lie just upstream of the put-in for this run. Head farther up Boulder Canyon on Highway 119 to scout out this action.

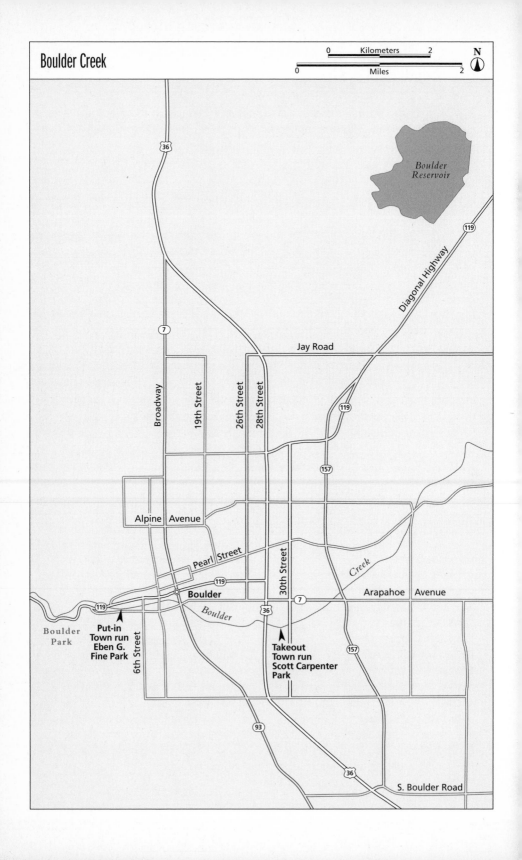

Boulder Creek

Whitewater in the middle of downtown Boulder.

5 Clear Creek

Draining the east side of the Continental Divide near Loveland Ski Area, Clear Creek is a larger drainage of the Front Range that offers plenty of whitewater action. The river starts off strong and fast as it makes it way rapidly downhill, all the while paralleled by highways. Paddlers come to Clear Creek for the action on the water—it is not for those seeking solitude or isolation.

Clear Creek Canyon, however, is a dramatic canyon that pulses with nearly continuous challenging advanced/expert whitewater. As the creek drops out of the mountains, it settles down and offers a gathering spot for Denver-area paddlers with the creation of a whitewater park in the foothills town of Golden. As Clear Creek continues east farther onto the Front Range plains, it flows into the South Platte River on the northern edge of Denver.

Lower Run

This bottom section of Clear Creek is the easiest and shortest after-work rinse-off for many Front Range advanced beginner/intermediate-level paddlers. Farther upstream, Clear Creek tumbles continuously over tight and technical advanced/expert-level rapids. Down here at the mouth of the canyon, just below harder whitewater, Clear Creek settles down to offer a cruisey quick paddle toward downtown Golden.

Steady current and small waves splash paddlers as they make their way down to the whitewater park. Numerous man-made ledges offer good surfing opportunities but also attract crowds of paddlers in the evenings when flows are good. The ledges are all straightforward charge-on-through affairs, albeit in more of a downstream mode than a playing mode.

A the far east edge of the whitewater park, one last hole—appropriately called Library Hole—is located next to the library. Shortly below here is the takeout, literally in downtown Golden.

Distance: 2.0 miles
Difficulty: Class II–III (advanced beginner/intermediate)
Craft: Kayaks
Approximate paddling time: 1 to 2 hours
Flows: 300 to 1,000 cfs
Season: April through July
Put-in: Just below Tunnel #1 Access
Takeout: Whitewater Park or Washington Street Bridge
Shuttle: To reach the takeout from downtown Golden, head north on Washington Street, cross over the creek, and turn left (west) at the next traffic light onto 10th Street. Head upstream to the parking area past the baseball fields; this is a higher takeout point.

To reach the put-in, return to the intersection of 10th and Washington Streets and turn left (north) onto Washington. Cross over Highway 58 and enter the highway heading west. Highway 58 becomes U.S. Highway 6 as it enters Clear Creek Canyon. Just below the first tunnel and below a diversion dam, look for a dirt pullout on the left-hand side; this is the put-in.

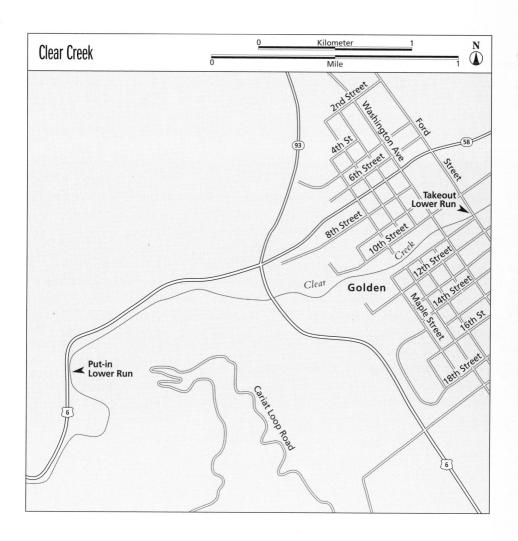

Clear Creek

Additional information: For playboaters the numerous man-made features of the white-water park (Class II), located at the takeout for this run, make for a great place to work on skills and meet other paddlers. A permanent slalom course is also set up through the top section of the park.

Miles of roadside advanced/expert sections (Class IV–V) lie upstream of this section on Clear Creek along US 6 and Interstate 70. Another good intermediate section can be found by putting in at Kermit's (US 6 and I-70 junction) and taking out at the put-in for the Black Rocks section.

6 South Platte River

Upstream of Denver, the South Platte River consists of two completely separate forks that offer multiple fine beginner to expert sections for paddling.

The North Fork comes to life as it flows off Kenosha Pass and gathers water from the central mountains with the outflow of the Roberts Tunnel Diversion. This diversion saps water from Lake Dillon and the Blue River and diverts it downstream under the mountains to quench Denver's thirst. As the North Fork flows downhill, it tumbles through a winding valley, the remote Bailey Canyon, and then through a lower narrow canyon before joining the South Fork.

Meanwhile, the South Fork has slowly come to life by flowing out of the Buffalo Peaks Wilderness Area. The top of the South Fork slides across the high open plateau of South Park before getting swallowed by multiple reservoirs. A it flows out of these upstream reservoirs, the South Fork tumbles through two distinct gorges—Eleven Mile and Cheesman—that offer fine intermediate/expert paddling. One more reservoir slows the South Fork before it is finally released, offering one last section of fine beginning paddling as it finally joins its North Fork.

With the North and South Fork flows finally joined, one last short section of advanced water in Waterton Canyon offers a glimpse of a lost canyon, submerged by construction of Chatfield Reservoir. Below this reservoir, the South Platte is urban but still offers some paddling options. The South Platte River finally comes together in the foothills above Denver. It then rolls out onto the Front Range plains of eastern Colorado before flowing into Nebraska, where it joins the North Platte River and ultimately flows into the Missouri River.

North Fork

Top Down section

This top section of the North Fork is rarely paddled, largely because of a noisy, busy highway that closely parallels the river and touchy private property issues in the valley. This section of river is literally born out of a tunnel just upstream of the put-in.

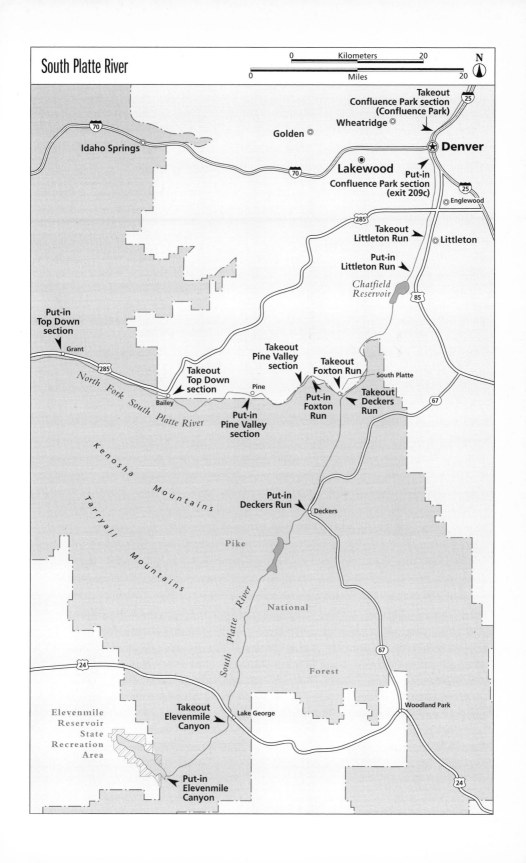

Water from the central mountains is diverted and released into this river channel in an attempt to quench the thirst of the Denver–Front Range area. The river offers some straightforward continuous intermediate whitewater and steady cold current throughout the length of this run. Respect the no trespassing signs. Flowing through a wide-open valley for most of this section, the river runs straight over a few small ledges, shallow rocks, small weirs, and through tight culverts on the way downstream. Be very cautious of man-made obstacles on this run and respect all private property.

Distance: 8.0 miles (shorter run possible)
Difficulty: Class II-III (intermediate)
Craft: Kayaks, canoes
Approximate paddling time: 2 to 4 hours
Flows: 250 to 500 cfs; dam controlled
Season: April through September; dam controlled
Put-in: Dirt pullout just downstream of Grant
Takeout: Dirt pullout upstream of Bailey
Shuttle: Use U.S. Highway 285 as the primary shuttle route along this section. To reach the takeout, head west out of the town of Bailey on US 285. Just upstream of town, look for a dirt pullout off of the highway where the road is next to the river; this is the takeout.

To reach the put-in, continue heading upstream (west) on US 285 to the small town of Grant just below the Roberts Tunnel Outlet. Look for a dirt pullout off the highway on the eastern edge of town; this is the put-in. Other pullouts off the highway afford additional access points to shorten the length of this run.

Pine Valley section

Flowing out of the isolated Bailey Canyon just upstream, the North Fork cruises into the rural pastures of Pine Valley. This run offers pleasant beginner water cruises past curious horses, as well as acres of private property. Slip on downstream through this wide valley while checking out craggy hillsides above the river bottom.

The top half of the run cruises in a swift manner until the bridge near Buffalo Creek. Downstream of this bridge, the North Fork slides back into a canyon and the whitewater picks up. Large granite boulders have fallen into the river channel near the hamlet of Ferndale, creating some technical maneuvering and rewarding rapids for intermediate paddlers. Steady current brings paddlers down to the takeout shortly below the crux of this section.

Distance: 10.0 miles (shorter run possible)
Difficulty: Top: Class I-II (beginner); bottom: Class II-III (intermediate)
Craft: Kayaks
Approximate paddling time: 3 to 4 hours
Flows: 250 to 500 cfs; dam controlled
Season: April through September; dam controlled
Put-in: Pine Valley Ranch Park
Takeout: Foxton
Shuttle: From the crossroads town of Pine Junction, located on US 285, go left (south) at the only traffic light and head downhill on Pine Valley Road (also known as County Road 126). At the bottom of the hill, turn right (west) at the T and head upstream into Pine Valley

Ranch Park; this is the put-in.

To reach the takeout, return to the T and continue heading downstream on Pine Valley/ Deckers Road. Just before crossing the river before the town of Buffalo Creek, turn left (northeast) onto Platte River Road (dirt). Head downstream to the town of Foxton; this is the takeout.

Additional information: You can put in at the town of Buffalo Creek to bypass the slower upstream 4.0 miles. Just upstream of this run is the advanced/expert Bailey Canyon (Class IV+)—a fine wilderness run that can be accessed by putting in just downstream of the town of Bailey.

Foxton Run

This piece of the North Fork offers a technical section of narrow rapids that navigate among large granite boulders. Just below the put-in, the river turns hard to the east and begins getting squeezed between tight, steep drops. Use extra caution through this section—scout and/or portage along the road on the left side of the river. Tight, challenging rapids course around boulders for the first half of the run. The bottom half tends to settle down and open up, providing gentler rapids and steady current down to the takeout.

Distance: 5.0 miles (shorter run possible)
Difficulty: Class II–III (intermediate)
Craft: Kayaks
Approximate paddling time: 2 to 3 hours
Flows: 250 to 500 cfs; dam controlled
Season: April through September; dam controlled
Put-in: Foxton
Takeout: Confluence–South Platte
Shuttle: Both the put-in and takeout, which are well marked, are accessed off Platte River Road (dirt). The road closely parallels the river on the left-hand side, providing good scouting while making the shuttle. To reach Platte River Road, take Foxton Road downhill off US 285 just outside the town of Conifer.

Additional information: Paddlers looking for a little less challenge can put in 2 miles above the confluence and find more Class II waters.

For the advanced paddlers out there, the abbreviated Waterton Canyon (Class IV) lies just downstream of the takeout for this run. This is an all-too-short paddle through a scenic little canyon with good whitewater before dumping into the backwaters of Chatfield Reservoir. A hike back up the river-left trail is required for this section's "shuttle."

South Fork

Eleven Mile Canyon

This scenic canyon is a top run on the South Fork of the South Platte and offers some great roadside intermediate paddling—in the off chance it actually is running. The releases coming out of Eleven Mile Reservoir are finicky and rare. But when there is sufficient water, this is a fine technical canyon for paddling some fun whitewater in a relatively out-of-the-way location with great camping along the river. Check out some expert rapids at the bottom of the canyon and up near the top of the canyon below the dam. Between these points is fine intermediate terrain that can easily be scouted while shuttling.

Distance: 7.0 miles (shorter run possible)
Difficulty: Class III (intermediate)
Craft: Kayaks, Canoes
Approximate paddling time: 2 to 3 hours
Flows: 200 to 400 cfs; dam controlled
Season: Rare; dam controlled
Put-in: Cove Campground
Takeout: Obrien Picnic Area
Shuttle: From Colorado Springs, head west on U.S. Highway 24 to Woodland Park and continue heading west to Lake George. Turn left (southwest) onto County Road 97, heading up Eleven Mile Canyon. The takeout is upstream of the bottom Class V whitewater, near the Obrien Gulch Picnic Area.

Continue heading upstream along the road, which closely parallels the river and affords great scouting. The put-in is below the top Class V whitewater, near Cove Campground.

Additional information: Bigger expert whitewater (Class V) lies upstream of the put-in and downstream of the takeout. The rarely run, expert-only Cheesman Canyon (Class V) lies downstream. This run requires some very technical paddling/portaging, as well as navigating tricky landowner issues.

Deckers Run

This lower section of the South Fork offers the best beginner/intermediate paddling between the big cities of Denver and Colorado Springs. Weekends can be a bit crowded with classes and club groups, but there are plenty of fun river miles for everyone. A road closely parallels the entire section, so it is easy to scout the whole section or to use numerous pullouts to shorten the overall length of this run.

The bottom half of the run contains more Class II whitewater action than the top half. The crux of this entire section is the Chutes Rapid (Class II–III)—a narrow chute between massive boulders located 2 miles above the confluence. The rest of this section is more open, with swift current, good eddylines, and splashy wave-train rapids. This is a great run for budding paddlers.

Distance: 11.0 miles (shorter run possible)
Difficulty: Class II–III (advanced beginner/intermediate)
Craft: Kayaks, canoes
Approximate paddling time: 3 to 4 hours
Flows: 250 to 500 cfs
Season: April through September; dam controlled
Put-in: Deckers
Takeout: Confluence of North and South Forks of the South Platte River

Shuttle: Use CR 97/Platte River Road as the primary route for shuttle for this section. To reach CR 97, take Highway 67 north from Woodland Park, just north of Colorado Springs. The put-in and takeout are well marked. Other access points can be used for intermediate points to shorten the overall length of this run.

Additional information: There is a fine section of intermediate-friendly Class III whitewater in the 3 miles just below Cheesman Dam to Deckers, but legal access for the put-in is challenging. The road goes away from the river, and there is lots of private property.

For the advanced paddler, the abbreviated Waterton Canyon (Class IV) lies just downstream of the takeout for this run. This is an all-too-short paddle through a scenic little canyon with good whitewater before dumping into the backwaters of Chatfield Reservoir. A hike back up the river-left trail is required for this section's "shuttle."

Littleton Run

This section of the South Platte lies just below Chatfield Reservoir as the river makes its way through the urban sprawl of Denver–Front Range. Riverside restoration and revitalization has taken hold along the South Platte through its metro corridor, so bike trails parallel parts of the river. Numerous, once deadly, dams have been modified to offer runnable chutes, but care still needs to be taken when approaching all manmade objects, of which there are many, along this section.

The real bonus of this urban run is that there is even some fine surfing at the takeout at Union Chutes. This comprises six or seven modified ledges that are up to Class III at good levels, so be sure to scout along the river trail on river-left.

Distance: 4.0 miles (shorter runs possible)
Difficulty: Class II-III (intermediate)
Craft: Kayaks, canoes
Approximate paddling time: 2 to 3 hours
Flows: 400 to 1,500 cfs; dam controlled
Season: Year-round
Put-in: South Platte Park, just below Chatfield Dam
Takeout: Bellview Avenue
Shuttle: To reach the takeout from downtown Denver, head south on Interstate 25. At exit 207, veer right (west) onto U.S. Highway 85, also known as Santa Fe Drive. After crossing Hampden and Oxford Avenues, look for Union Avenue; turn right (west) and cross the river. Turn immediately right and park on the eastern edge of the baseball fields next to the river—

this is the takeout.

To reach the put-in, return to US 85; turn right (south) and continue heading upstream. Just after crossing Mineral Avenue, look for South Platte River Park. Turn right (west) into the park and wind toward the parking area next to the river—this is the put-in.

Additional information: Flatwater touring enthusiasts can enjoy a tour on Chatfield Reservoir, located just upstream of this section. Refer to the lake-touring section of this guide for further information.

Playboaters may wish to spend more time paddling and surfing the numerous ledges at Union Chutes Park—all of which can be scouted and accessed off the river trail on river-left near Union Avenue off US 85.

Confluence Park Section

This lower urban run on the South Platte features a few more river miles down to a great river play park known as Confluence Park—named for the confluence of the South Platte River and Cherry Creek right in the heart of downtown Denver. Since this section is farther downstream in the middle of a major metro area where all storm drains—as well as various other pollutants—run into the river, the water quality down here can be a bit more suspect.

Christie Dobson enjoys an afternoon surf session at Union Chutes.

Low flows and flatwater greet paddlers at the put-in for this section. Just downstream, water is diverted back into the river channel, and flows are increased. Paddlers will also find a runnable chute over the Zuni Dam, 0.5 mile below the put-in. Cruisey water brings paddlers down to the top of Confluence Park—a series of ledges and waves that offer good urban surfing or fun crash-on through rapids.

Scouting can be done on the river-right bike trail along the river. This is a really nice riverside gathering spot for city-trapped outdoor enthusiasts, with viewing decks, trails, and a fine swimming spot. Enjoy the best paddling in the middle of Denver.

Distance: 3.0 miles (shorter runs possible)
Difficulty: Class II–III (intermediate)
Craft: Kayaks, canoes
Approximate paddling time: 1 to 3 hours
Flows: 400 to 1,500 cfs; dam controlled
Season: Year-round
Put-in: Eighth Avenue boat launch
Takeout: Confluence Park
Shuttle: To reach the put-in, use exit 209C off I-25 and follow signs for the Eighth Avenue boat launch; this is the put-in.

To reach the takeout, head north on the river frontage road that parallels the river on the left. Or get back on I-25, get off at exit 210B, and head north to park along the river next to the REI store; this is the takeout.
Additional information: Paddlers seeking to work on just their playboating skills may wish to spend time just at the man-made drops and surf waves located at the takeout in Confluence Park next to the REI store.

7 Arkansas River

The Arkansas is the best-known river for paddling in the entire state—and the busiest rafting river in the entire West. With more than 125 miles of paddling options, ranging from Class I to Class V, the Ark offers something for every paddling skill level. The Arkansas Valley, located in the center of the state, is a very scenic setting for paddling as it cuts between the Saguache Mountains to the west (home to Mount Elbert, the tallest mountain in Colorado) and the Mosquito Mountain Range to the east.

Snow-covered 14,000-foot peaks flank the skyline on the upper sections of the river, while craggy granite boulders line the banks and form the major obstacles within the river channel. As the Ark flows southward through the valley, various sections provide thrilling intermediate/advanced paddling options. The scenery is very nice and rural feeling. As the Ark makes an eastward bend below the town of Salida, the lower river canyon is closely paralleled by U.S. Highway 50 and offers some fine roadside intermediate paddling options.

Just upstream of Canon City, the Ark is severely squeezed into the dramatic and claustrophobic advanced/expert run through the Royal Gorge. As the Ark is finally spit out from the towering canyon walls, it settles down and offers some fine beginner paddling options down toward Pueblo. Just upstream of town, the Ark is dammed, forming Lake Pueblo, which offers a fine flatwater touring route. Below the dam that forms the reservoir, the Ark offers up another beginner section to just above the recently constructed Pueblo Whitewater Park. Below the whitewater park, the Ark slows down even further as it dumps out onto the eastern plains of Colorado before flowing into Kansas.

Headwaters Section

This top section of the Arkansas is high-altitude, shallow, cold, fast water that appeals more to wading fishermen. It does offer some fine beginning miles and can be added onto the Granite Gorge section below as a longer beginner/intermediate run. Snow-covered peaks tower above the western skyline, and the swift current quickly carries paddlers downstream.

The highway closely parallels the length of this run, so it is easy to see what you are getting into. Below the small hamlet of Balltown, at the confluence of Lake Creek that flows out of Twin Lakes, the flow of the Arkansas increases and becomes more of a real river, with a steadier current that quickly brings paddlers down to the takeout.·

Arkansas River

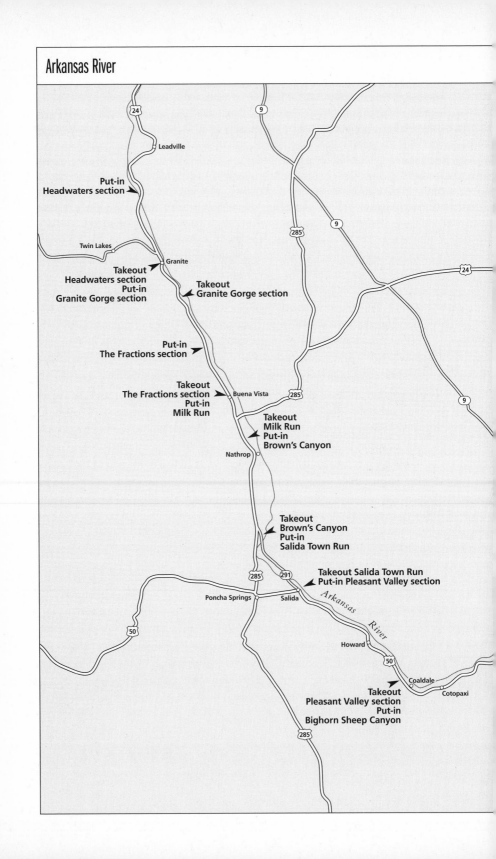

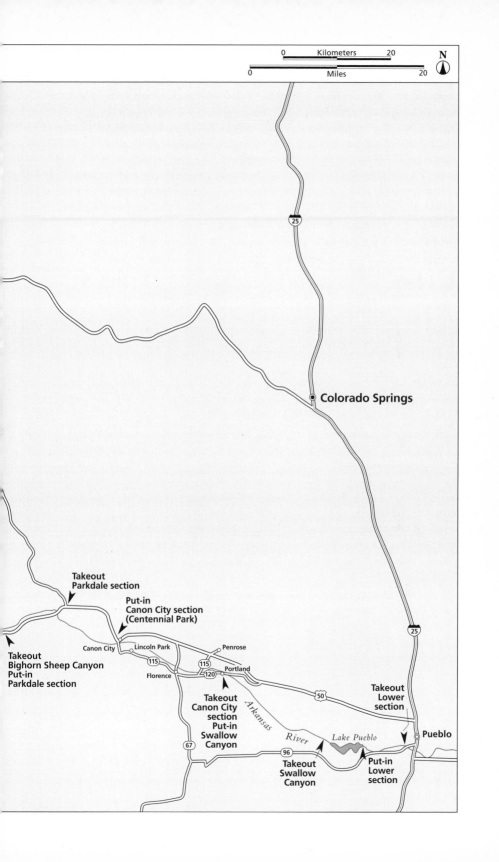

Distance: 10.0 miles (shorter runs possible)
Difficulty: Class I–II- (beginner)
Craft: Canoes, kayaks, rafts
Approximate paddling time: 3 to 4 hours
Flows: 300 to 1,000 cfs
Season: April through August
Put-in: Hayden Meadows river access
Takeout: Bridge in Granite
Shuttle: Use U.S. Highway 24 for both the put-in and takeout. The put-in is located south of Leadville on US 24. Heading south, the highway crosses the river. The recreation site just after the bridge on the right side of the river is the put-in.

To reach the takeout, continue heading downstream to the small town of Granite. Recreation area signs on the left (east) side of the highway indicate the takeout.

Additional information: Balltown can be used as a higher put-in for the Granite Gorge section below. This gives paddlers a couple more miles of pleasant beginner/easy intermediate current to warm up.

Granite Gorge Section

Below the put-in, the Arkansas quickly slides into a forested canyon that is tucked away from the highway. Intermediate paddlers will encounter Class III whitewater a mile below the put-in. Tight riverbanks and midstream granite boulders choke the current and offers good waves.

Be aware of an old dam below the early whitewater—it can be portaged on the right. Below the dam, one more short canyon squeezes the river down once again, offering some good waves and straightforward rapids. Pine Creek Rapid lies just below the takeout, so be sure to catch a good eddy well upstream of the entrance to the chaos below.

Distance: 4.0 miles
Difficulty: Class II–III (intermediate)
Craft: Canoes, kayaks, rafts
Approximate paddling time: 1 to 2 hours
Flows: 300 to 2,000 cfs
Season: April through August
Put-in: Bridge in Granite
Takeout: Just above Pine Creek Rapid
Shuttle: Use US 24 for both the put-in and takeout. The put-in is located in the small town of Granite. Look for a pullout on the east side of the highway just downstream of a bridge across the river.

To reach the takeout, head south on US 24 for approximately 4 miles. Look for a large dirt pullout on the east side of the highway. Park here and follow a short, rough jeep trail leading down to railroad tracks that parallel the river.

Additional information: This is a mandatory takeout for paddlers not wishing to tackle the advanced/expert runs of Pine Creek (Class V) and the Numbers (Class IV) just downstream.

The Fractions sections

Putting in just below the tail end of the Numbers section, the Fractions is a fine run of intermediate paddling that is a considerable step down in difficulty from the upstream runs. This piece of river offers fine Class II–III whitewater with numerous boulders to maneuver around. The steady gradient creates constant current through this run that will keep intermediate paddlers on their toes—choppy waves are found throughout. This very enjoyable run ends at the busy boat ramp in Buena Vista.

Distance: 7.0 miles
Difficulty: Class II–III (advanced beginner/intermediate)
Craft: Canoes, kayaks, rafts
Approximate paddling time: 2 to 3 hours
Flows: 400 to 2,200 cfs
Season: April through August
Put-in: Railroad Bridge Recreation Site
Takeout: Buena Vista boat ramp
Shuttle: From Main Street in downtown Buena Vista, look for signs for County Road 371; take this north out of town. The paved road eventually turns to dirt, crosses the river, and closely parallels the river on its left side. Look for signs for Railroad Bridge Recreation Site; this is the put-in.

To reach the takeout, return to downtown and the Main Street intersection. Turn left (east) and follow Main Street until it dead-ends in a park. This recreation site is the takeout.

Additional information: For paddlers seeking to work on their playboating skills, the run downstream from the boat ramp at the takeout 0.25 mile to South Main provides multiple man-made features to practice surfing. If you're playing below the takeout, a river trail on river-right provides hiking access back upstream to the boat ramp.

Milk Run

This section of river starts with some funs waves and rapids along the South Main river corridor. Try some surfing, or just charge straight on through. Heading downstream a mile or so below the put-in, paddlers will encounter an old dam that must be run on the right (Class III). Except for this hazard, the rest of the run settles down into fine, busy Class II paddling through a more open section of the valley that is tucked away from the highway.

Distance: 12.0 miles (shorter run possible)
Difficulty: Class II–III (beginner/intermediate)
Craft: Canoes, kayaks, rafts
Approximate paddling time: 3 to 5 hours
Flows: 400 to 2,200 cfs
Season: April through August
Put-in: Buena Vista boat ramp
Takeout: Fisherman's Bridge
Shuttle: Use U.S. Highway 285 to access both the put-in and takeout.

Additional information: Easier beginner paddling can be found by putting in at the US 285/24 bridge in Johnson Village and heading down to the takeout at Fisherman's Bridge. Another option is to take out farther downstream at Ruby Recreation Site. (See the Brown's Canyon description below for more information.)

Brown's Canyon

This is one of the most popular whitewater runs in the entire United States. A combination of rugged canyon scenery lined with ponderosa and piñon pines; challenging but not life-threatening pool-drop rapids; and straightforward logistics makes Brown's a classic intermediate day trip. Private paddlers will enjoy the whitewater on this run, but they will have to share it with lines of commercial rafts in the summertime.

Lined with granite boulders, the Ark slides into the canyon with Canyon Doors (Class III) and Pinball Rapid (Class III). The action continues below with Zoom Flume (Class III), Big Drop (Class III), and Widowmaker (Class III). In parts of the canyon, swirly water and strong eddylines can create a larger challenge than just crashing through the waves.

The rapids are frequent, with good pools below each one where paddlers can regroup and clean up any pieces or savor some of the low-walled canyon scenery. With steady current and adrenaline-fueled smiles, paddlers will find their way to the popular takeout at Hecla Junction with relative ease.

For those wishing to complete the canyon, Seidel's Suckhole (Class III+) and Double Drop (Class III) lay farther downstream. After these big boys, the Arkansas eases down and flows out of Brown's Canyon to the lower takeout. Brown's really is a classic that must be paddled if you're in the area.

Distance: 14.0 miles (shorter run possible)
Difficulty: Class III (intermediate)
Craft: Canoes, kayaks, rafts
Approximate paddling time: 3 to 5 hours
Flows: 400 to 2,200 cfs
Season: April through August
Put-in: Fisherman's Bridge
Takeout: Highway 291 bridge
Shuttle: Use US 285 and Highway 291 to access both the put-in and takeout. To reach the put-in, head north from Nathrop on US 285 and look for signs for Fisherman's Bridge on the east side of the highway. Cross the river, park in the lot on river-left, and hike down to the launching point.

To reach the takeout, head south on US 285 through Nathrop. Shortly after Nathrop, look for a sign for Hecla Junction River Access on the left (east) side of the highway. This is an intermediate access and the most popular takeout.

To access the lower takeout, keep heading south on US 285 and turn left (east) onto Highway 291 toward Salida. Just before the highway crosses the river, turn left (north) into a dirt parking lot and access point.

Additional information: To shorten the overall length of the run, paddlers can put in at Ruby Mountain Recreation Site, which is downstream of Fisherman's Bridge and closer to the actual entrance to the canyon. This bypasses a couple of miles of Class II water. Most paddlers use the higher takeout point at Hecla Junction off US 285. Using both of these shorter access points, the length of the run is closer to 8.0 miles.

◀ *Chad and Stephanie Crabtree style their way downstream on the Fractions.*

Salida Town Run

This nice little beginner section offers a fine way to paddle into town. The river channel stays open as it passes ranchland and cruises swiftly downstream around smaller rocks and through splashy waves. One small dam marks the only real hazard on this run, and a runnable channel has been created on the left for paddlers to navigate over the dam. Other than the dam, cruisey paddling takes you right into downtown Salida, where multiple man-made surf waves offer fine playboating at the takeout.

Distance: 9.0 miles (shorter run possible)
Difficulty: Class II (beginner/intermediate)
Craft: Canoes, kayaks, rafts
Approximate paddling time: 2 to 3 hours
Flows: 500 to 2,700 cfs
Season: April through August
Put-in: Highway 291 bridge
Takeout: Riverside Park, F Street in downtown Salida
Shuttle: The main street in downtown Salida is F Street. To reach the takeout, stay on F Street heading north until it runs into the river; this is the takeout.
To reach the put-in, turn around and follow

F Street south to First Street. Turn right (west) onto First Street and drive out of town, heading upriver. First Street becomes Highway 291; follow the highway for 8 miles. When Highway 291 crosses over the river, turn right (north) into the river access parking lot and put-in.
Additional information: A lower put-in can be accessed at Big Bend Access off US 285 south; this will cut 3.0 miles from the paddle. For paddlers seeking to work on their playboating skills, the boat ramp just upstream of F Street in Salida provides multiple man-made features to practice surfing.

Pleasant Valley section

The Ark begins bending to the east as it drops through a nice rural valley just downstream of Salida. Beautiful views of the Sangre de Cristo Mountains fill the south skyline and open grasslands, and occasional cottonwood trees line the riverbanks. Bear Creek Rapid (Class III) is located 3 miles below the put-in. Another good one is Badger Creek Rapid (Class III), just downstream from the Rincon river access point. Other than these two rapids, the rest of the run is steady current mixed with pleasant Class II whitewater.

Molly Cumming and Kim Garner enjoy the classic scenery and whitewater of Brown's Canyon. ▶

Distance: 18.5 miles (shorter run possible)
Difficulty: Class II–III (advanced beginner/intermediate)
Craft: Canoes, kayaks, rafts
Approximate paddling time: 3 to 5 hours
Flows: 500 to 2,700 cfs
Season: April through August
Put-in: Riverside Park, F Street in downtown Salida
Takeout: Vallie Bridge Recreation Site

Shuttle: From the put-in off F Street in downtown Salida, head north 2 blocks on F Street and turn left (west) onto First Street. Follow First Street out to the junction with U.S. Highway 50; turn left (east) on US 50 and follow it downstream approximately 18 miles.

Additional information: A higher takeout point is sometimes used at the Rincon river access, located just upstream of the town of Howard. This will cut 4.0 miles off the paddle.

Bighorn Sheep Canyon

This section of the river is also known as the Lower Arkansas River Gorge. The river leaves the open valley upstream and slides back into a craggy, granite-boulder gorge that closely parallels US 50. Most everything can be scouted while running shuttle, so you will see what you're getting into before putting in. Private paddlers will have to share this section with the hordes of commercial rafters on a midsummer day.

The upper portion of the run is a bit slower, but the action picks up below Texas Creek. The rapids of note on this section are Cottonwood, Little Cottonwood, Texas Creek, Maytag, and Devil's Hole—all Class III water. In all, this is a fine roadside intermediate run.

Distance: 20.0 miles (shorter runs possible)
Difficulty: Class III (intermediate)
Craft: Kayaks, rafts, canoes
Approximate paddling time: 5 to 7 hours
Flows: 500 to 2,700 cfs
Season: April through August
Put-in: Vallie Bridge Recreation Site
Takeout: Pinnacle Rock Recreation Site

Shuttle: Both the put-in and takeout are well marked on US 50, heading downstream east of Salida.

Additional information: Lone Pine Recreation Site below the town of Cotapaxi has been used as an intermediate access point on this section. Other roadside pullouts are also available.

Parkdale Section

This section is a bit like the upstream run, but with a bit more condensed whitewater. Once again, US 50 offers fine scouting while shuttling so that you see everything you'll be paddling before actually putting in. The big ones on this section are Three Rocks (Class III), Five Points (Class III), Spikebuck (Class III+), and the Tube (Class III). This is another fine roadside intermediate level run and not to be missed if you're driving east on US 50.

Distance: 8.0 miles
Difficulty: Class III (intermediate)
Craft: Kayaks, rafts, canoes
Approximate paddling time: 2 to 4 hours
Flows: 500 to 2,700 cfs
Season: April through August
Put-in: Pinnacle Rock Recreation Site
Takeout: Parkdale Recreation Site

Shuttle: Both the put-in and takeout are well marked on US 50, heading downstream east of Salida.

Additional information: You don't want to miss the takeout—just downstream lies the grand entrance into advanced/expert Royal Gorge (Class IV+).

Canon City Section

As the Ark comes out of Royal Gorge, it finally enters into the land of the beginning paddler. This section is a gentle, meandering river lined with cottonwoods set beneath dry rolling hillsides above. The first beginner section is located right in Canon City, heading downstream swiftly with fine current through a bit of urban-ness.

Be wary of high water on this run—paddlers can be swept toward bridge abutments and driftwood piles. The major hazard on this section is a low head dam located 4 miles below the put-in that must be portaged on the left. Fear not; the portage is short and easy. This section is a fine beginner run, with steady current and fun choppy waves rather than just a flatwater paddle.

Distance: 15.0 miles (shorter run possible)
Difficulty: Class I–II (beginner)
Craft: Canoes, kayaks, rafts
Approximate paddling time: 3 to 5 hours
Flows: 500 to 2,500 cfs
Season: April through August
Put-in: Centennial Park in Canon City
Takeout: Highway 120 bridge next to the cement plant in Portland
Shuttle: Use US 50 as the primary shuttle route for this section. From the middle of Canon City, take US 50 west and look for signs for Centennial Park directly across from the train depot. Turn left (south), cross the river, and pull into the western end of the park close to the boat ramp; this is the put-in.

To reach the takeout, return to US 50 and head east out of town. Near the town of Penrose, look for signs for Highway 115. Turn right (south) onto Highway 115; eventually cross the river and come to a T. Turn left (east) at the T onto Highway 120 and head downstream to the tiny town of Portland. The road crosses the river next to an old cement plant; this is the takeout.

Additional information: An intermediate access point is sometimes used at the Highway 67 bridge in the town of Florence. Below this point is fine, urban-free beginner paddling.

Swallow Canyon

Beginning paddlers will find a surprisingly remote and nature-filled section through the Lower Arkansas as it slices through Swallow Canyon. This is a great open canoe section, where easy, gentle water greets paddlers along with a tranquil setting. Rolling gray limestone and shale canyon walls climb 200 feet up from the river, while cottonwood groves line the banks. These stands are home to eagles, great blue herons, and ospreys. Migrating ducks and geese also take refuge in this secluded canyon. The last 2 miles or so will be a flatwater slog as you drop into the backwaters of Lake Pueblo to reach the takeout.

Distance: 10.0 miles
Difficulty: Class I (beginner)
Craft: Canoes, kayaks, rec boats
Approximate paddling time: 3 to 4 hours
Flows: 500 to 2,500 cfs
Season: April through August
Put-in: Highway 120 bridge next to the cement plant in Portland
Takeout: Northshore Marina, Pueblo Reservoir
Shuttle: To reach the put-in, head east out of Canon City on US 50. Near the town of Penrose look for signs for Highway 115. Turn right (south) onto Highway 115; eventually cross the river and come to a T. Turn left (east) at the T onto Highway 120 and head downstream to the tiny town of Portland. The road crosses the river next to an old cement plant; this is the put-in.

To reach the takeout, return to US 50 and continue heading east. Approaching Pueblo West, look for McCulloch Boulevard. Turn right (south) onto McCulloch Boulevard and follow it around as it eventually enters Lake Pueblo State Park. Pay the entrance fee and, once in the park, follow signs for Northshore Martina; this is the takeout.

Additional information: For a flatwater/lake tour while in the area, check out Pueblo Reservoir (see the Lake Pueblo description).

Lower Section—Dam to Nature Center

One last river run on the Arkansas offers a fine in-town beginner run. The Dam to Nature Center run is nearly flat, with no real rapids to speak of. Along the way downstream, there are a few small weirs to negotiate that are easily paddled over; they also create some nice little surfing opportunities. Even at higher flows, this is a fairly tame trip that is great for beginners and kids. This is both an excellent early-season warm-up run and a great way to get the whole family on the water.

Distance: 7.0 miles
Difficulty: Class I–II (beginner)
Craft: Canoes, kayaks, rec boats
Approximate paddling time: 2 to 3 hours
Flows: 450 to 2,000 cfs
Season: April through August
Put-in: Picnic area below Lake Pueblo Dam
Takeout: Nature center
Shuttle: The put-in is located at a picnic area just inside Lake Pueblo State Park off Highway 96 just west of Pueblo. Enter the park through the gate leading to the north portion of the park. A parks pass is required to park at the picnic grounds. Once past the gate, make the first right onto a road leading to a parking lot at the picnic area.

To reach the takeout, return to Highway 96 and head back east into town. At the intersection of Pueblo Boulevard and West 11th Street is Nature Center Road. The Pueblo Nature Center is located at the end of Nature Center Road. The boat ramp upstream of the deck on river-left is the take-out.

Additional information: For those with just one vehicle, there's a paved bicycle trail the entire length of this run, making bike shuttling very easy.

For paddlers seeking to work on their playboating skills, Pueblo Whitewater Park lies just downstream of the takeout (one dam must be portaged). The park offers multiple man-made features over 0.25 mile to practice surfing and playing.

8 Rio Grande

Yes, this is *that* Rio Grande. Perhaps one of the most famous rivers in the West, the Rio Grande start way up high in the southwest corner of Colorado. At 1,887 miles, the second-longest river in the United States, it drains the north side of the San Juan Mountains and makes a wide southeastern arc as it eventually tumbles out of the mountains. It then cuts through the plateaus of New Mexico before snaking along the Texas-Mexico border on its way into the Gulf of Mexico.

Up here in Colorado, the Rio Grande is a fine river for paddling, with good beginner/intermediate sections for canoeists, kayakers, and rafters. The top section is a short, remote canyon lined with jagged rocks and towering fir trees. As it eases downstream through a broad valley, the river passes willow and cottonwood trees. As the Rio Grande drops into the broad San Luis Valley, the gradient drops to next to nothing and the flow begins to get sucked through irrigation diversions that are used for farming.

Stay west of the valley to find some fine paddling—and to say you actually paddled the headwaters of the Rio Grande.

Headwaters Box Canyon

Box Canyon truly is the highest paddled section of the Rio Grande. Just 2 miles below the Rio Grande Reservoir, the river cuts into a very nice steep-walled canyon filled with good technical whitewater. The setting is one of a remote jagged canyon

with a committing little gorge that is almost 1,000 feet deep with heavily forested (spruce and fir) hillsides.

Take care navigating the rocky rapids down in here—you are a long way away from a road. Once through the canyon, paddlers drop out onto a broad open valley for the last 3.0 miles down to the takeout.

Due to the irregular releases of the dam just upstream, finding this section with enough flow can be the biggest challenge of the whole run. Nevertheless, this section is recommended for its beauty and thrilling whitewater.

Distance: 9.5 miles
Difficulty: Class III (intermediate)
Craft: Whitewater kayaks, canoes
Approximate paddling time: 3 to 5 hours
Flows: 200 to 500 cfs; dam controlled
Season: May through June; dam controlled
Put-in: River Hill Campground
Takeout: Fern Creek Bridge
Shuttle: Head west out of the town of Creede on Highway 149 for approximately 25 miles. Turn left (west) onto River Hill Road (Forest Service Road 520). Climb uphill and stay on FSR 520, passing Road Canyon Reservoir. Look for signs for River Hill Campground; this is the put-in.

To reach the takeout, return down the hill to the junction of FSR 520 and Highway 149. Turn right (east) and head downvalley for 3 miles. Turn right (south) onto Forest Service Road 522 and follow it to a bridge crossing the river; this is the takeout.

◀ *A young kayaker thoroughly enjoys the fun surf waves on the Dam to Nature Center run on the Lower Arkansas.*
Courtesy of Bryan Kelsen Photography

Rio Grande

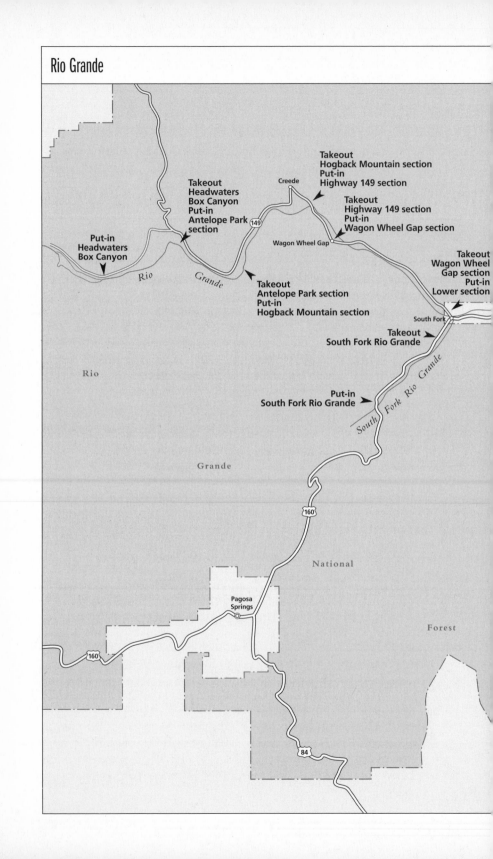

Creede

Put-in
Headwaters
Box Canyon

Takeout
Headwaters
Box Canyon
Put-in
Antelope Park
section

Takeout
Hogback Mountain section
Put-in
Highway 149 section

Takeout
Highway 149 section
Put-in
Wagon Wheel Gap section

Wagon Wheel Gap

Takeout
Wagon Wheel
Gap section
Put-in
Lower section

Takeout
Antelope Park section
Put-in
Hogback Mountain section

South Fork

Takeout
South Fork Rio Grande

Put-in
South Fork Rio Grande

Rio

Grande

South Fork Rio Grande

Rio

Grande

National

Forest

Pagosa
Springs

160

160

84

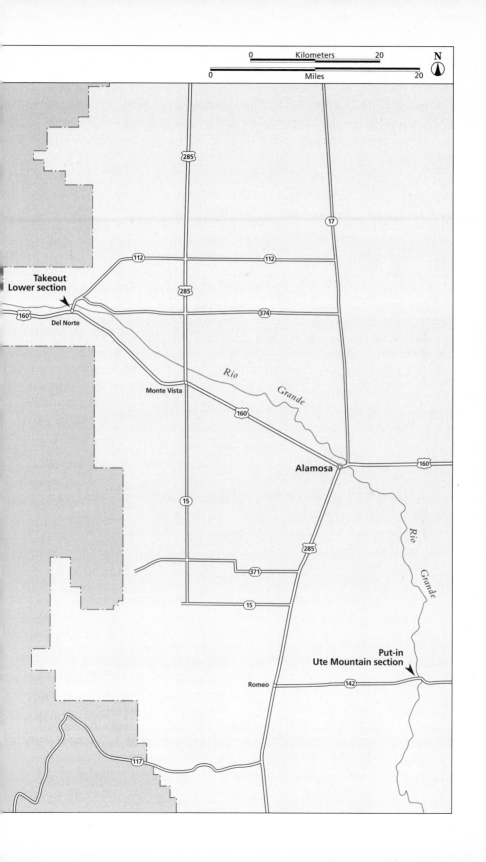

Antelope Park Section

This section of the Rio Grande offers beginning paddlers a pleasant afternoon float through a meandering broad open valley. There is little of interest on the water in terms of difficulty, although the wide-open sky and lush valley are scenic enough to keep a paddler's interest. Private ranches line much of the riverbanks through here, so be aware of this if you need to step ashore for any reason.

Distance: 9.0 miles
Difficulty: Class I-II- (beginner)
Craft: Kayaks, canoes, rafts
Approximate paddling time: 3 to 4 hours
Flows: 300 to 800 cfs
Season: April through July
Put-in: Fern Creek Bridge
Takeout: Hogback Mountain
Shuttle: Head west out of the town of Creede on Highway 149 for about 22 miles. Turn left (south) onto FSR 520 and follow it to a bridge crossing the river; this is the put-in.

To reach the takeout, return to Highway 149. Turn right (east) and head downvalley to Marshall Park Campground. Cross a bridge just after this campground and turn right (south) onto Forest Service Road 523. Follow this dirt road back upstream on the right side of the river. Stay to the right at the junction with Lime Creek Road. Shortly after this junction, FSR 523 is very close to the river; this is the take-out, directly across from Hogback Mountain.

Hogback Mountain Section

This section of the Rio Grande cuts into a shallow canyon as it drops out of its upstream broad open valley. Paddlers will find a nice fir-lined canyon with some fun technical Class II whitewater that can grow to easy Class III in highest flows.

There is a slightly remote feeling in here, and paddlers will enjoy numerous wave trains and pleasant scenery away from the road on the upper portion of this run. On the lower part of this section, the river mostly parallels Highway 149, so the seclusion is gone. If you want to opt out of this section, intermediate access points can be used to shorten your paddle.

Distance: 15.0 miles
Difficulty: Class II-III- (advanced beginner/intermediate)
Craft: Whitewater kayaks, canoes, rafts
Approximate paddling time: 4 to 6 hours
Flows: 300 to 800 cfs
Season: April through July
Put-in: Pullout off FSR 523
Takeout: Highway 149 bridge
Shuttle: To reach the put-in from Creede, head west on Highway 149. Turn left (south) onto FSR 523 just before crossing the river and follow this dirt road upstream on the right side of the river. Stay to the right at the junction with Lime Creek Road. Shortly after this junction, FSR 523 is very close to the river; this is the put-in, directly across from Hogback Mountain.

To reach the takeout, return to Highway 149 and head back east toward Creede. Go into town, staying on Highway 149. On the east side of town, the highway crosses the river; the takeout is at the bridge.

Additional information: Other takeout points can be used to shorten the run, including the first Highway 149 bridge and the Fivemile Bridge west of Creede.

Highway 149 Bridge to Wagon Wheel Gap

This short section of the Rio Grande is another wide-open pastoral paddle like the Antelope Park section farther upstream. The river settles down, with swift current through here but no whitewater of any kind. The valley is broad and flat, as horses and private ranches line the riverbanks.

Distance: 5.0 miles
Difficulty: Class I-II- (beginner)
Craft: Kayaks, canoes, rafts
Approximate paddling time: 1 to 2 hours
Flows: 300 to 800 cfs
Season: April through July
Put-in: Highway 149 bridge
Takeout: Phipps Bridge just above Wagon Wheel Gap

Shuttle: Heading east out of Creede, Highway 149 crosses the river; this is the put-in.

To reach the takeout, continue heading downstream (east) on Highway 149 to the next bridge, located at Wagon Wheel Gap; this is the takeout.

Wagon Wheel Gap Section

This nice little section of paddling begins in a steep V-shaped valley that is almost 2,000 feet deep. The tighter valley walls squeeze the river, and the current picks up speed and offers fine Class II whitewater in the top half of this run. Caution is needed in navigating a few bridges shortly below the put-in—pilings in narrow spaces can present a challenge in higher water.

The V-shaped valley eventually opens up and the current settles down a bit as it eases down toward South Fork. Highway 149 closely parallels the length of this section, so paddlers can scout while doing the shuttle.

Distance: 12.0 miles
Difficulty: Class II (advanced beginner/intermediate)
Craft: Whitewater kayaks/canoes, rafts
Approximate paddling time: 3 to 4 hours
Flows: 300 to 800 cfs
Season: April through July
Put-in: Wagon Wheel Gap

Takeout: Highway 149 bridge, South Fork
Shuttle: Highway 149, which parallels the length of this section, is used for both the put-in and takeout.
Additional information: Palisade Campground can also be used as an intermediate access point to create a shorter run.

South Fork Rio Grande

This tight, technical little tributary to the Rio Grande offers some fine intermediate paddling when the water levels are right. This whole run can be scouted while driving down U.S. Highway 160 from Wolf Creek Pass heading east. Heavily forested hillsides cloak a nice section of paddling that also offers busy, technical, and shallow whitewater. Because of its small riverbed, this one becomes too low to paddle early, so catch it when you can.

Distance: 9.0 miles
Difficulty: Class II–III- (intermediate)
Craft: Whitewater kayaks, canoes
Approximate paddling time: 2 to 3 hours
Flows: 250 to 400 cfs
Season: May through June
Put-in: Park Creek Campground
Takeout: Beaver Creek Road bridge
Shuttle: Use US 160, which parallels the majority of this section, for both the put-in and the takeout access points. Heading west out of South Fork, you'll see a sign for Beaver Creek Road off to the left (east) next to a bridge crossing the river; this is the takeout.

To reach the put-in, continue heading west on US 160 for 9 miles, looking for a Forest Service sign for Park Creek Campground. Turn left (east) into the campground; this is the put-in.

Lower Section

As the Rio Grande drops out of the upstream mountains and begins to enter the flat valley below, it offers one last section of worthy beginner paddling. This lower section offers paddlers nice current and good riffles with small waves; numerous Class I–II- rapids are scattered throughout the run.

This section is also noted by the Colorado Division of Wildlife for its gold-medal trout (browns mostly) fishing. Numerous drift boats ease their way downstream below South Fork.

Distance: 18 miles
Difficulty: Class I–II- (beginner)
Craft: Kayaks, canoes, rafts
Approximate paddling time: 4 to 6 hours
Flows: 300 to 1,000 cfs
Season: April through September
Put-in: Highway 149 bridge, just west of South Fork
Takeout: River park just upstream of the Highway 112 bridge in Del Norte
Shuttle: To reach the put-in, from the junction of Highway 149 and US 160 in South Fork, head west on Highway 149 to the first bridge over the river; this is the put-in.

To reach the takeout, return to the junction of Highway 149 and US 160 and head east on US 160 to Del Norte. In the middle of town, turn left (north) at the traffic light onto Highway 112. Just after crossing some railroad tracks, look for a park off to the left (west). Pull in here and park next to the river; this is the takeout.

Additional information: Shorter runs are possible by using Hanna Lane/Highway 17 (turn north) off US 160 as a midrun access point.

An upstream view from the rim of the lower section of the Ute Mountain run of the Rio Grande in New Mexico.

Ute Mountain Section

Just before the Rio Grande crosses from Colorado into New Mexico, the river begins cutting its way down into the northern edge of the Taos Plateau and offers a fine beginning-level overnight trip. At the southern edge of the San Luis Valley, the Rio Grande picks up some once-diverted flow from irrigation in the form of numerous side streams. There is adequate water for paddling, as well as a fine high-desert canyon worth exploring.

Below the put-in, a beautiful basalt rock gorge rises up 200+ feet as the river drops down beneath the walls. This section is considered the northern part of the Taos Gorge Wild and Scenic River. Abundant birdlife can be spotted throughout the run—the canyon is home to eagles, falcons, owls, mergansers, and Canada geese. Numerous fun Class II rapids are scattered throughout this run, but they tend to increase as paddlers make their way downstream.

Two days is ample time to float through this section, and paddlers can call numerous fine campsites on narrow benches home for the night. This out-of-the-way segment is seldom run, so paddlers will most likely have this section of river all to themselves.

Distance: 24.0 miles
Difficulty: Class I–II- (beginner)
Craft: Kayaks, canoes
Approximate paddling time: 2 days
Flows: 500 to 2,000 cfs
Season: April through June
Put-in: Lobatos Bridge
Takeout: Lee Trail (New Mexico)
Shuttle: To reach the put-in, head south from Fort Garland on Highway 159 through the town of San Luis. Continue heading south approximately 10 miles and look for H Road. Turn right (west) on H Road toward the town of Mesita. Pass through town and turn left (south) onto 7 Road. Shortly turn right (west) onto G Road and follow it to the bridge that crosses the river; this is the put-in.

To reach the takeout, return to Highway 159. Turn right (south) and cross into New Mexico. Colorado Highway 159 becomes New Mexico Highway 522. Ten miles south of the border, turn right (west) onto Sunshine Valley Road. Follow this dirt road underneath power lines for 6 miles toward the canyon rim. Next to the canyon rim, turn left (south) and go 4 miles to the trailhead for Lee Trail. Lee Trail requires a grueling 500-yard-long, 200+-foot climb, and paddlers must carry all their gear and boats up the trail to the actual takeout.

Additional information: Just downstream from this run lies the expert-only Upper Taos Box Run (Class V), followed by Lower Taos Box Run (Class III–IV).

9 Conejos River

The Conejos River (*conejos* means "rabbit" in Spanish) flows in a relatively isolated part of the state on the east side of the South San Juan Mountains below the Continental Divide. Largely draining the mountains to the south of Wolf Creek Pass, the Conejos does not lack for ample flows come snowmelt time of year. But given that it is also a relatively small drainage, the flows on the Conejos tend to run out by June in most years.

The river begins with the outflow of Platoro Reservoir near its headwaters; this dam is largely used for flood control. Below here the river courses steeply and tightly through some expert whitewater before easing down into a short intermediate canyon, finally settling down into milder sections as it eases out of the mountains and into the flat San Luis Valley before joining the Rio Grande.

The Conejos River corridor is an isolated area of the state surrounded by national forest. Paddlers will find heavily forested hillsides and little traffic when paddling and camping in the area. This area is indeed worthy of Wild and Scenic status. This little-disturbed pocket of the state is home to pristine forests and abundant wildlife, including bald eagles, peregrine falcons, and bighorn sheep.

Pinnacle Gorge

This short but sweet canyon is located where the road climbs up and away from the river. Paddlers encounter a brief isolated section of technical river running through a deep grotto of fluted volcanic ash spires, thus the name Pinnacle Gorge. The crux of the run is found in the middle of the run at the base of the largest spires—this is Pinnacle Rapid (Class III). Two miles below the rapid, the canyon walls settle back and the river eases out of the gorge. The takeout is located at the mouth of the canyon.

Distance: 5.0 miles
Difficulty: Class II–III (intermediate)
Craft: Whitewater kayaks, canoes, rafts
Approximate paddling time: 2 to 3 hours
Flows: 250 to 600 cfs
Season: April through June

Put-in: Bridge on Lake Fork Road
Takeout: Bridge on County Road 250 just upstream of the South Fork confluence
Shuttle: Dirt CR 250, which parallels the course of the river, provides both the put-in and takeout access points for this section.

Middle Valley Section

Still set in a pleasant valley, this section of the Conejos lacks the dramatic gorge and whitewater of the upstream run. Largely a cruisey paddle, this section offers good current but little whitewater to speak of. Mellow paddling here carries paddlers past large ranches and easy country living.

Be wary of private property along the river through here, as well as the possibility of barbed wire.

Distance: 12.0 miles
Difficulty: Class I–II (beginner)
Craft: Kayaks, canoes, rafts
Approximate hiking time: 3 to 5 hours
Flows: 300 to 800 cfs
Season: April through June
Put-in: Bridge on CR 250 just upstream of South Fork confluence
Takeout: Highway 17 bridge
Shuttle: Use dirt CR 250, which parallels the course of the river for the length of this section, to reach the put-in.

To reach the takeout, head downstream (east) on County Road 250 to the junction with Highway 17. Turn right (south) onto Highway 17 and travel a short distance to the bridge that crosses the river; this is the takeout.
Additional information: Spectacle Lake Campground can be used as an intermediate access point to shorten the length of this run.

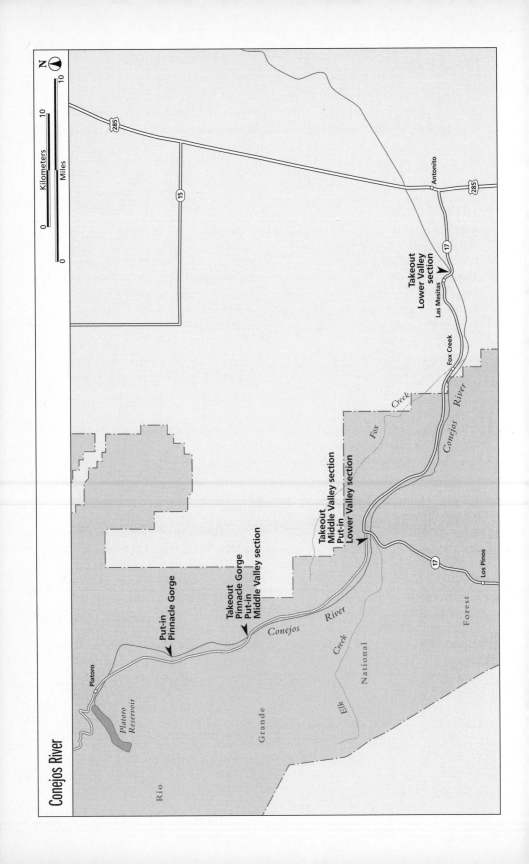

Conejos River

Lower Valley Section

Gaining a good bit of flow from the entrance of Elk Creek just upstream of the put-in, this lower section of the Conejos holds more water longer into the summer. What paddlers will find down here near the bottom of the river canyon is a mellow paddle that passes by ranches and is paralleled by Highway 17 for the length of the run. Good water and current push paddlers downstream with little effort.

The crux of this run is S-Turn Rapid, just upstream of Aspen Glade Campground. Paddlers may wish to scout this rapid while running shuttle. Except for this larger rapid, the rest of the run is straightforward, offering one last section of pleasant paddling on the Conejos before it flattens out into the valley below.

Distance: 7.0 miles
Difficulty: Class I-II (beginner/intermediate)
Craft: Whitewater kayaks, canoes, rafts
Approximate paddling time: 2 to 4 hours
Flows: 300 to 800 cfs
Season: April through July
Put-in: Highway 17 bridge
Takeout: Mogote Campground

Shuttle: Use Highway 17, which parallels the length of this section, for both the put-in and takeout. All access points are well marked.
Additional information: Aspen Glade Campground can be used as an intermediate access point. The river at this campground is also the site of S-Turn Rapid, the largest scoutable rapids on this section.

The Conejos Valley is home to great camping, rewarding fishing, and pleasant paddling.
Courtesy of William Luster Photography

Western Slope Paddles

(North-South)

A group of paddlers enjoys pleasant paddling and sandstone cliffs on the Ruby/Horsethief section of the Colorado River.

10 Yampa River

The Yampa River is the longest free-flowing tributary in the Colorado River Basin. The Yampa flows out of the east side of the Flat Tops and the northern flank of the Gore Range before eventually joining the Green River along the Colorado-Utah border. Dropping out of the mountains in this northern part of the state, the Yampa flows strong with snowmelt in late spring/early summer and settles down as lower flows in mid- to late summer continue dropping.

The highest runs on the Yampa are set in a pleasant open valley with a pastoral setting before cutting through the ski town of Steamboat Springs. Downstream of town, the Yampa swallows up the Elk River and meanders lazily downstream through more ranchland toward the town of Craig. Downstream of Craig, the river slides into isolated and scenic Duffy Canyon and the short Juniper Canyon; both offer some fine canoeing. Downstream of these canyons, the Yampa lazes through an open valley before getting a dramatic pinch through the expert-only Cross Mountain Gorge. After exiting this slice of a canyon, the Yampa cruises through Lily Park and the Little Snake River enters, further increasing the flow.

Below Lily Park, the Yampa drifts into a gem of a multiday trip through the impressive Yampa Canyon. This section does not disappoint desert wilderness lovers who also seek a little bit of whitewater. At its confluence with the Green River in Echo Park, the Yampa is officially swallowed up beneath dramatic Steamboat Rock as the Green rolls downstream into Whirlpool Canyon in Dinosaur National Park.

Above-Town Section

This top section of the Yampa is a cruisey, meandering float above town set in a wide fertile valley. You'll be passing numerous meadows, horse pastures, and private land, so be very mindful of private property issues along this section of the river. Paddlers will see willows along the riverbanks, as well as frequent wildlife and birdlife, as this piece of the Yampa smoothly and slowly heads downstream toward town.

Distance: 8.0 miles (shorter run possible)
Difficulty: Class I (beginner)
Craft: Canoes, kayaks
Approximate paddling time: 2 to 4 hours
Flows: 300 to 1,400 cfs
Season: April through July
Put-in: Highway 131 bridge
Takeout: Yampa River Park, Rich Weiss Memorial Park
Shuttle: From downtown Steamboat Springs, head south on U.S. Highway 40 out of town. Turn right (west) onto Highway 131 and continue heading south. After a few miles, look for a river access site near a bridge over the river; this is the put-in.

To reach the takeout, return to US 40 and head toward downtown. Before actually entering the downtown area, look for signs for Yampa River Park off the left-hand (west) side of the highway; this is takeout.

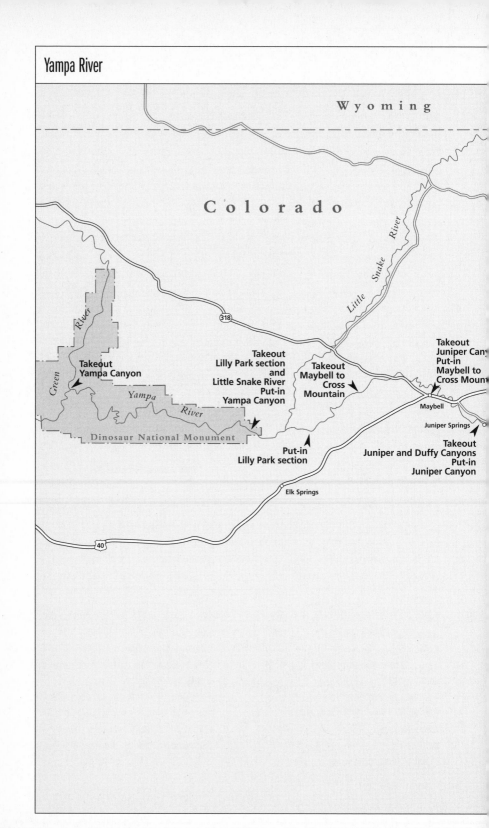

Wyoming

Colorado

Little Snake River

318

Green River

Takeout
Yampa Canyon

Yampa River

Dinosaur National Monument

Takeout
Lilly Park section
and
Little Snake River
Put-in
Yampa Canyon

Takeout
Maybell to
Cross
Mountain

Put-in
Lilly Park section

Takeout
Juniper Can
Put-in
Maybell to
Cross Moun

Maybell

Juniper Springs

Takeout
Juniper and Duffy Canyons
Put-in
Juniper Canyon

Elk Springs

40

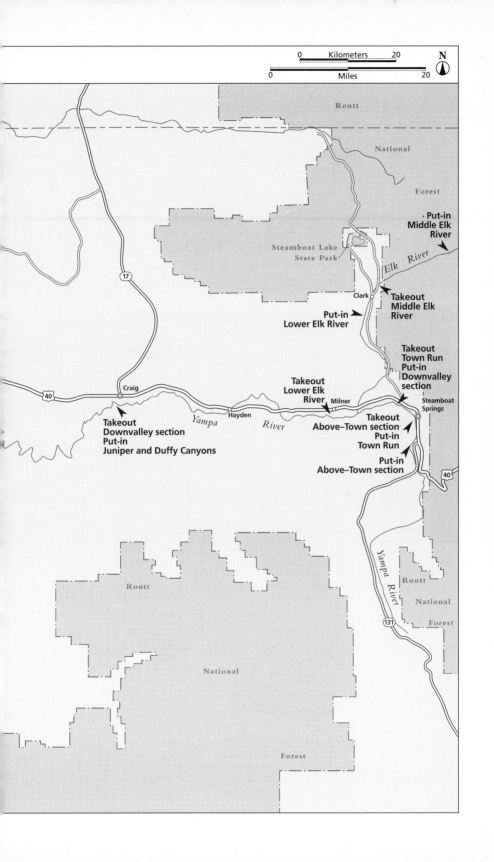

Additional information: A shorter (3.0-mile) section is sometimes paddled down to the normal takeout by using a put-in at the River Road bridge. Another section farther upstream can also be paddled. This rarely done upper section offers another 15.0 miles of Class I water. Please respect all private property signs in this area.

C-Hole is the site for great surfing on the lower end of the Town Run.

Town Run

The Yampa through the middle of Steamboat Springs has become a river-restoration success story. The Yampa River Improvement Project was implemented in 1981 in an attempt to improving the river corridor and the quality of paddling through town by placing boulders in various locations in the river channels. What was once a mellow section has now become a playful and enjoyable paddling run for the after-work crowd. More recent river improvements include construction of a permanent slalom course and man-made play features. There really is something for every type of paddler on this section.

Distance: 2.0 miles
Difficulty: Class II–III- (beginner/intermediate)
Craft: Canoes, kayaks, rafts
Approximate paddling time: 1 to 3 hours (depending on playing)
Flows: 300 to 1,400 cfs
Season: April through August
Put-in: Yampa River Park, Rich Weiss Memorial Park
Takeout: 20 Mile Road bridge next to the library
Shuttle: Use US 40 as the main shuttle route on this section. From the put-in on the south end of downtown, head north through the middle of town. On the west side of town, turn left (south) onto 20 Mile Road, looking for signs for the library. A parking area is located on the downstream side of the bridge; this is the takeout.

Additional information: A permanent slalom course has been set up in the river-right channel at the put-in. For paddlers seeking the best playboating opportunities, check out the man-made play spots of C-Hole and D-Hole next to the takeout. A bike path and paved streets make a bike shuttle an easy shuttle option.

Elk River

Middle Elk River

Just downstream of Steamboat Springs, the Elk River flows out of the Mount Zirkel Wilderness Area and heads to the south before joining the Yampa on the west side of town. Another swift, free-flowing, snowmelt-fed river, the Elk tumbles in a more continuous character over boulders in a heavily wooded canyon. No major drops greet paddlers, just fast eddyless boogie boating in higher water.

Distance: 8.5 miles
Difficulty: Class III (intermediate)
Craft: Kayaks
Approximate paddling time: 2 to 3 hours
Flows: 600 to 1,800 cfs
Season: May through July
Put-in: Box Canyon Campground
Takeout: Bridge in Clark
Shuttle: From downtown Steamboat Springs, head west on US 40 past the library. Look for signs for County Road 129; turn right (north) onto CR 129 and travel upstream to the town of Clark. Just above town, CR 129 crosses the river; this is the takeout.

To reach the put-in from the takeout, turn right (east) onto Forest Service Road 400 (dirt) and follow it upstream along the river. Look for signs for Box Canyon Campground; this is the put-in.

Additional information: The Upper Elk River lies just upstream of the put-in, offering a short but nonstop expert-only section of Class IV–V whitewater.

Lower Elk River

This bottom section of the Elk is a meandering float set in a wide fertile valley. Passing numerous meadows, horse pastures, and private land, please be very mindful of private property issues along this section of the river. The Elk lazes along this rural river bottom mostly away from roads in a slow-paced valley.

Distance: 20.0 miles (shorter run possible)
Difficulty: Class I–II (beginner)
Craft: Canoes, kayaks
Approximate paddling time: 2 to 3 hours
Flows: 600 to 1,800 cfs
Season: May through July
Put-in: Clark
Takeout: Milner
Shuttle: Use CR 129 as the primary route for access along this section. From downtown Steamboat Springs, head west on US 40 past the library. Look for signs for CR 129; turn right

(north) onto CR 129 and travel upstream to the town of Clark. Just above town, CR 129 crosses the river; this is the put-in.

To reach the takeout, return to the junction of CR 129 and US 40. Turn right (west) onto US 40 and take it out of town. Look for a river access area near the US 40 bridge just upstream of the town of Milner.

Additional information: A higher takeout is sometimes used at the junction of CR 129 and the Mad Creek confluence. The trailhead parking area here is a takeout.

Downvalley Section

This section of the Yampa is a meandering, snaking run set alongside US 40 in a pleasant valley. Because of the private property and proximity to the highway, this section is sought after for its beginner-level floating opportunities and its float fishing, rather than for remoteness or wilderness. This segment marks the transition of the Yampa from a mountain river flowing past fir and evergreens to one flowing into a more barren desertlike landscape by the takeout. It can also be characterized as floating from condos to cattle ranches.

Throughout this section, the river runs through a wide-open valley set with grassy meadows at the foot of surrounding mountains. The river itself is flat and picks up quite a bit of current in highest flows, but otherwise it is a straightforward, rapidless section of beginner water.

Distance: 50.0 miles (shorter runs possible)
Difficulty: Class I (beginner)
Craft: Canoes, kayaks, rafts
Approximate paddling time: Depends on length of run
Flows: 1,000 to 5,000 cfs
Season: April through August
Put-in: 20 Mile Road Bridge, next to the library
Takeout: South Beach river access
Shuttle: Use US 40 as the primary route for access along this section. To reach the put-in, from downtown Steamboat Springs, head toward the west side of town. Turn left (south) onto 20 Mile Road and look for signs for the

library. The parking area on the downstream side of the bridge is the put-in.

To reach the takeout, head west on US 40 downstream to the town of Craig. Once in downtown Craig, continue heading west and just out of town. Look for signs for Highway 13. Turn left (south) onto Highway 13 and head downstream toward the takeout at the South Beach river access site.

Additional information: Other intermediate access points are the Double Bridges access and Yampa River State Park; both are just west of the town of Hayden on US 40.

Juniper and Duffy Canyons

This section offers beginning paddlers a fine remote segment of river that cuts into steep-walled sandstone canyons. This is a gem of a run for desert-loving, multi-day-seeking canoeists set in a 500+-foot-deep canyon. Below the put-in, the river eases past numerous cottonwood flatlands that provide excellent campsites. Wildlife abounds, with numerous sightings of mule deer, bighorn sheep, nesting eagles, ospreys, and waterfowl.

The river through the canyon meanders beneath steeps walls but offers no whitewater and is a rare canyon section with no real threat. The river slides out of the canyon and for the last 10 miles flows through open, barren lands before the takeout at the bridge in the now abandoned town of Juniper Springs.

Distance: 45.0 miles (shorter run possible)
Difficulty: Class I (beginner)
Craft: Canoes, kayaks, rafts
Approximate paddling time: 2 to 4 days
Flows: 1,000 to 5,000 cfs
Season: April through August
Put-in: South Beach river access
Takeout: Juniper Springs
Shuttle: To reach the put-in, head west on US 40 downstream to the town of Craig. Once in downtown Craig, continue heading west and just out of town. Look for signs for Highway 13. Turn left (south) onto Highway 13 and head downstream toward the put-in at the South Beach river access site.

To reach the takeout, return to the junction of Highway 13 and US 40. Head west on US 40, looking for a sign for County Road 53. Turn left (south) onto this dirt road and drive until you reach a bridge over the river at abandoned Juniper Springs; this is the takeout.

Additional information: A higher takeout is often used at the Duffy river access off County Road 17 (located off US 40), which is located upstream on river-right from Government Bridge.

A river permit is required to paddle this section of river. Please use minimum-impact camping skills (toilet system and fire pan) to help protect the river corridor from future degradation.

Juniper Canyon

This short but very dramatic section of the Yampa cuts a V-shaped slot through Juniper Mountain. Measuring 1,500 feet deep, Juniper is another little-known but rewarding beginner-level paddling run. Squeezed between canyon walls, numerous small Class II rapids are found in the bottom of this canyon. Previous blasting has formed a Class III rapid 2 miles into the run. This short, attractive canyon is far from any people; it is little paddled and will offer a fine, remote day on the water.

Distance: 5.0 miles
Difficulty: Class II (advanced beginner)
Craft: Canoes, kayaks, rafts
Approximate paddling time: 2 to 3 hours

Flows: 1,000 to 5,000 cfs
Season: April through August
Put-in: CR 53 bridge at Juniper Springs
Takeout: River access at US 40 bridge

Shuttle: Use County Road 74 (dirt) as the primary route for access on this section. To reach the takeout, head east on US 40 from the town of Maybell. At the first US 40 bridge, look for the designated river access on the south side of the highway; this is the takeout.

To reach the put-in, continue heading east on US 40 to CR 74. Turn right (east) onto CR 74 and follow it down to the bridge crossing the river in Juniper Springs; this is the put-in.

Additional information: This section of river is often added onto the upstream run of Duffy and Juniper Canyons to provide a total of 50 miles of fine canoeing.

Maybell to Cross Mountain

This slow, meandering float wanders peacefully in a rural valley past rolling hills, meadows, and open ranchland that is rarely paddled. The river is calm and passes numerous ranches with lazy horses. Paddlers typically head upstream to the canyon runs just above to seek more remote paddling than this section has to offer.

Distance: 30.0 miles (shorter run possible)
Difficulty: Class I (Beginner)
Craft: Canoes, kayaks, rec boats
Approximate paddling time: Depends on length of run
Flows: 1,000 to 5,000 cfs
Season: April through August
Put-in: River access at US 40 bridge
Takeout: Entrance to Cross Mountain Gorge
Shuttle: Use US 40 as the primary access route for this section. To reach the put-in, head east on US 40 from the town of Maybell. At the first US 40 bridge, look for the designated river access on the south side of the highway; this is the put-in.

To reach the takeout, head west on US 40 through town for an additional 16 miles to County Road 85 (dirt). Turn right (north) and bounce down the dirt road, staying to the right until you eventually pull up next to the river; this is the takeout.

Additional information: Intermediate access points are available at the County Road 19 and Highway 318 bridges just east of Sunbeam.

Lily Park Section

This gentle section of the Yampa is a pleasant paddle squeezed between the dramatic Cross Mountain Gorge upstream and the renowned Yampa Canyon downstream. Between these two gorges, the Yampa cruises through a nice out-of-the-way valley that offers a fine day of paddling for beginners. This is an open valley set in sagebrush country, with proud sandstone bluffs and buttes in the distance. The river offers gentle current through here and no rapids. Higher spring runoff creates a faster paced float down to the takeout.

Distance: 17.0 miles (shorter run possible)
Difficulty: Class I (beginner)
Craft: Canoes, kayaks, rafts
Approximate paddling time: 3 to 5 hours
Flows: 1,000 to 5,000 cfs
Season: May through July
Put-in: Exit of Cross Mountain Gorge
Takeout: Deerlodge Park
Shuttle: To reach the put-in, head west out of Maybell on US 40 for 17 miles. Turn right (north) onto Deerlodge Park Road. Drive 4 miles and look for a parking area on the right just below the exit to Cross Mountain Gorge; this is the put-in.

To reach the takeout, continue heading downstream on Deerlodge Park Road until you reach the launch site at Deerlodge Park; this is the takeout.

Additional information: An intermediate access point is available at the County Road 25 bridge. The short but sweet, expert-only Cross Mountain Gorge (Class IV-V) lies just upstream of the put-in.

Little Snake River

The Little Snake is the most unknown beginner river in the whole state of Colorado. Tucked way up in the northwest corner away from everybody, and with only a narrow window of good flows because it's free flowing, the Little Snake hardly sees paddlers. That is the very reason to go. Not only does the river lack people but it is also relatively remote in terms of a scenic multiday paddling experience for canoeists.

Flowing south through the Little Snake State Wildlife Area in its upper reaches, the river eventually joins the Yampa in the middle of Lily Park. It largely meanders peacefully through a lush fertile bottomland lined with willows and cottonwoods set beneath rolling sagebrush hills. Out-of-the-way ranches can be seen along the banks, and rough dirt roads somewhat parallel sections of the river. This is a fine, isolated little river for adventurous canoeists seeking to explore a little-known treasure.

Distance: 60.0 miles (shorter run possible)
Difficulty: Class I (beginner)
Craft: Canoes, kayaks
Approximate paddling time: 2 to 4 days
Flows: 500 to 1,500 cfs
Season: May through June
Put-in: County road bridge southwest of Baggs, Wyoming
Takeout: Deerlodge Park launch site
Shuttle: To reach the put-in from the town of Craig, head north on Highway 13. Just before the Wyoming-Colorado state line, south of Baggs, turn left (west) onto County Road 430. Follow CR 430 downstream as it parallels the river for 26 miles until it crosses the river; this is the put-in.

To reach the takeout, return to the town of Craig and head west out of town on US 40, continuing through the town of Maybell. Sixteen miles west of Maybell, turn right (north) onto Deerlodge Park Road. Follow Deerlodge Park Road to its end and look for signs for the Deerlodge Park launch site; this is the takeout.

Additional information: Another intermediate, and more-used, access point is the Highway 318 bridge, just west of Maybell.

Sheer sandstone cliffs dwarf paddlers at Echo Park near the confluence of the Yampa and Green Rivers.

Yampa Canyon

Yampa Canyon offers the beginner/intermediate an ideal combination of paddling characteristics—an incredibly beautiful canyon setting, typically good water levels, numerous days of paddling, low gradient, gentle straightforward rapids, and great camping. The only problem with paddling this section of river is actually getting permission to put in. A river permit is required, as assigned by the Dinosaur National Park Service River Permits Office. The permit process is a lottery that must be applied for well before the intended launch date. Get many folks in your group to apply, and hope for the best.

Once you've obtained a permit, settle in for a wilderness paddling experience like only a few other rivers in the entire United States. Yampa Canyon delights largely due to its beauty from put-in all the way to its takeout. The canyon itself is more than 2,000 feet deep and is filled with twists and turns as it navigates around sheer-walled cliffs that literally drop right down into the river, dwarfing paddlers who paddle beneath them.

The river cruises away from the put-in and drops into the canyon just below. The whitewater found here includes Tepee (Class II+) and Big Joe Rapids (Class II+). The big one of the trip is Warm Springs Rapid (Class III+), which can be scouted, or portaged on the right. Numerous side canyons offer fine hiking options, and assigned camping usually ensures a great campsite for the evening. At the confluence with the Green River in Echo Park, the Yampa is swallowed up. A remote takeout is located just below here on the right.

Distance: 46.0 miles
Difficulty: Class II–III+ (advanced beginner/intermediate)
Craft: Canoes, kayaks, rafts
Approximate paddling time: 3 to 4 days
Flows: 700 to 8,000 cfs
Season: April through July
Put-in: Deer Lodge Park
Takeout: Echo Park
Shuttle: Use US 40 as the primary route for access on this section. To reach the put-in, head 16 miles west of Maybell on US 40. Turn right (north) onto Deerlodge Park Road and follow this road to its end. Look for signs for the Deerlodge Park launch site; this is the put-in.

To reach the takeout, return to US 40 and head west, crossing into Utah and looking for signs to Dinosaur National Park. Turn right (north) into the park, pay the entrance fee, and follow signs for the Split Mountain Boat Ramp; this is the takeout.

Additional information: Yampa Canyon paddlers often add the downstream Whirlpool and Split Mountain Canyon sections of the Green River for an additional 25 miles of paddling. A river permit is required to launch on this section of the Yampa and the Green Rivers. For more information about obtaining a river permit, go to www.nps.gov/dino/river.

11 Green River

The Green River is a classic river of the West first explored by John Wesley Powell in the late 1800s. Flowing southward out of the impressive Wind River Mountain Range—a beautiful, relatively little-known mountain landscape in southwestern Wyoming—the Green is unfortunately stopped in its tracks by Flaming Gorge Dam. The outflow of Flaming Gorge offers paddlers a stretch of good beginner/intermediate water as the Green slides into Red and Swallow Canyons and eventually out through the broad plains of Browns Park.

The Green slices back into the rugged mountainside by forming the challenging but beautiful Lodore, Whirlpool, and Split Mountain Canyons. These fine multiday river trips can be linked together to offer a classic intermediate paddling trip with great canyon scenery. The Green really makes a transition as it begins a due-south course, flowing through the more barren high-desert canyons of Desolation, Grey, Stillwater, and Labyrinth Canyons before ultimately joining the Colorado River in the heart of Canyonlands National Park.

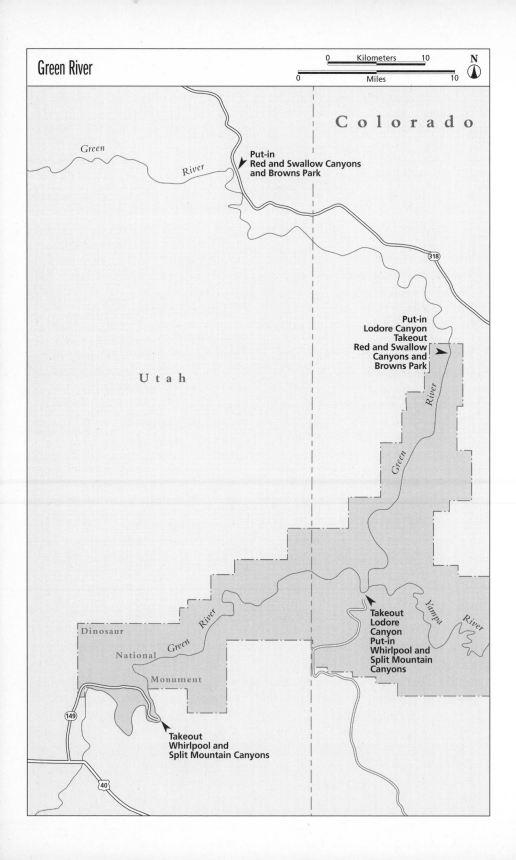

Green River

Kilometers 0 — 10

Miles 0 — 10

N

Colorado

Green River

Put-in
Red and Swallow Canyons
and Browns Park

318

Utah

Put-in
Lodore Canyon
Takeout
Red and Swallow
Canyons and
Browns Park

Green River

Green River

Yampa River

Takeout
Lodore
Canyon
Put-in
Whirlpool and
Split Mountain
Canyons

Dinosaur

National

Monument

149

Takeout
Whirlpool and
Split Mountain Canyons

40

Red and Swallow Canyons and Browns Park

Red Canyon is located just below the Flaming Gorge Dam and is a fine intermediate section. The cold water (because of the outflow from the bottom of the reservoir) offers fine float-fishing and can become quite crowded with fishing dory boats.

The river swiftly cruises between steep iron oxide–colored walls that stand over 1,500 feet above the river. Good fishing, easy access, and nice scenery make Red Canyon a popular run. Below here the river opens up a bit and then eventually drops back between the walls of Swallow Canyon. Within the canyon walls, paddlers encounter Red Creek Rapid (Class II+), the rowdiest whitewater found upstream of Lodore Canyon. Below the excitement of Swallow Canyon, the river opens up in a broad plain and eases down to Class I all the way to the lowest access point.

Distance: 46.0 miles (shorter runs possible)
Difficulty: Class I-II (beginner)
Craft: Canoes, kayaks, rafts
Approximate paddling time: 1 to 3 days
Flows: 800 to 4,000 cfs
Season: April through July
Put-in: Spillway boat ramp below Flaming Gorge Dam (Utah)
Takeout: Lodore boat launch
Shuttle: From Maybell head west on Highway 318, crossing over the Little Snake River. Eventually come to the turnoff on County Road 34N for the Lodore boat launch area; this is the takeout.

To reach the put-in and additional upstream access points, continue heading west on Highway 318. At the Utah-Colorado state line, the road turns to dirt. Continue upstream, passing the Swallow Canyon boat launch area (either a put-in or lower takeout). Five miles farther up the road is the Bridge Hollow access point. Go 9 more miles upstream through the town of Dutch John to signs for the river access below Flaming Gorge Dam; this is the highest put-in.

Additional information: Shorter runs can be done by using the Little Hole boat ramp (Mile 7), Bridge Hollow access point (Mile 16), Swallow Canyon boat ramp (Mile 26), or the full distance down to Lodore.

Lodore Canyon

Lodore offers some challenging intermediate paddling in the bottom of an incredibly beautiful remote and deep sandstone-walled river canyon. This canyon offers some of the most challenging whitewater on the entire Green River as it flows southward to its eventual confluence with the Colorado River in the middle of Canyonlands National Park in southern Utah. Unfortunately its power has largely been controlled and regulated by Flaming Gorge Dam farther upstream from the put-in. Nonetheless, the canyon scenery and still-thrilling rapids make Lodore a fine multiday river trip.

The canyon walls jump up just below the launch site and squeeze paddlers throughout this trip down to the confluence with the Yampa River. Side canyons offer intimate little grottos tucked away from the main canyon. Through the canyon the whitewater provides good short rapids such as Upper Disaster Falls, Lower Disaster, and Triplet

Kayakers line up for fine surfing in the middle of Lodore Canyon below Hell's Half Mile.

Falls (all Class III) and Hell's Half Mile (Class III+). Most of these rapids require technical rock maneuvering at lower water levels, with good recovery pools below. Hell's Half Mile, as the name implies, is a longer rapid without a good run out.

Below here the canyon walls still stand tall, but the river swiftly heads downstream beneath Steamboat Rock and takes in the Yampa River tributary in the Echo Park area of Dinosaur National Park. This river also is regulated by the Park Service and requires a river permit. Just brave the process—your reward will be launching on this fine section of river.

Distance: 20.0 miles (longer run possible)
Difficulty: Class III (intermediate)
Craft: Canoes, kayaks, rafts
Approximate paddling time: 2 to 4 days
Flows: 800 to 2,000 cfs
Season: Dam controlled; higher flows May through June; low flows (800 cfs) September through October
Put-in: Lodore boat ramp

Takeout: Echo Park, Dinosaur National Park
Shuttle: To reach the put-in from Maybell, head west on Highway 318 for approximately 45 miles. Look for County Road 34N (dirt) off to the left (south) and signs for the Lodore Canyon launch site. Follow this road down to the river, looking for a boat ramp and campground; this is the put-in.

To reach the takeout, return to Maybell

and take U.S. Highway 40 west. Just east of the town of Dinosaur, turn right (north) into Dinosaur National Park. Pay the entrance fee and head north on the scenic Harpers Corner Road. Turn right onto Sand Canyon Road (dirt) and follows signs for Echo Park. Wind down the hillside to the river bottom and look for a boat ramp and camping area; this is the takeout.

Additional information: A Lodore Canyon river trip often continues downstream by adding the Whirlpool and Split Mountain Canyon sections of the Green River for a total distance of 45.0 miles. A river permit is required to launch on this section of the Green River. Check www.nps .gov/dino/river for river permit information.

Whirlpool and Split Mountain Canyons

The Green offers two more canyons of fine intermediate-level paddling through Whirlpool and Split Mountain Canyons. Just below the put-in downstream of the Yampa River confluence, the Green drops into the dramatic entrance to deep, dark Whirlpool Canyon. As the name implies, swirly water and eddylines bounce off the canyon walls forming unstable paddling through numerous Class II rapids and Greasy Pliers Rapid (Class III).

As the Green slides abruptly out of this canyon, it enters the lazy open valley known as Island Park. After 7.0 miles of open, tranquil water, the Green suddenly plummets straight into a mountain, thus cutting Split Mountain Gorge. Down here the whitewater picks up with straightforward rapids with big waves in the form of Moonshine (Class III), S.O.B. (Class III-), School Boy (Class II+), and Inglesby Rapids (Class III-). The canyon rim towers above the river, and all too soon paddlers are spit out onto the boat ramp that is the takeout. If combined with farther upstream runs on the Green (Lodore) or on the Yampa, you have just concluded one of the best intermediate multiday river trips in the United States.

Distance: 25.0 miles (shorter run possible)
Difficulty: Class III (intermediate)
Craft: Canoes, kayaks, rafts
Approximate paddling time: 2 days
Flows: 800 to 3,000 cfs
Season: Dam controlled; May through July
Put-in: Echo Park
Takeout: Split Mountain boat ramp (Utah)
Shuttle: Use US 40 as the primary route for access on this section. Just east of the town of Dinosaur, turn right (north) into Dinosaur National Park. Pay the entrance fee and head north on the scenic Harpers Corner Road. Turn right onto Sand Canyon Road (dirt) and follows signs for Echo Park. Wind down the hillside to

the river bottom and look for a boat ramp and camping area; this is the put-in.

To reach the takeout, return to US 40 and head west, crossing into Utah and looking for signs for Dinosaur National Park. Turn right (north) into the park, pay the entrance fee, and follow signs for the Split Mountain boat ramp; this is the takeout.

Additional information: It is possible to paddle just the 8.0-mile-long Split Mountain Canyon as a day trip. A river permit is required to launch on these sections of the Green River. Check www.nps.gov/dino/river for river permit information.

12 White River

The little-known White River starts high up in the Flat Tops Wilderness north of Glenwood Springs and flows a long way west out of the state before joining the Green River in Utah. Two forks of the White tumble out of the mountains—the North and South Fork—and their combined flows provide a short but good paddling season on the downstream runs.

The downstream sections of the White River all offer fine beginning canoeing sections, while adventurous expert kayakers have found paddling up on the forks. The area around the White is a sparsely populated and vegetated landscape; and there is a very rural, ranchy, and lazy feeling to this part of the state. Known largely for its oil and gas exploration, the area surrounding the White has been saturated with natural gas wells, and the future looks bleak for wilderness preservation in the area.

The real gem of paddling the White is the last canyon the river tucks into below the town of Rangely as it drops down toward its confluence with the Green River. Away from the roads, the bottom canyon of the White offers a fine multiday flatwater canoe trip through a nice little canyon. There is a flavor of cows and oil rigs around, but the Lower White is worth a trip if you're looking for an out-of-the-way, sparsely paddled section of river.

Confluence to Meeker

This top section of the White offers a small river for some paddling within a very narrow window of adequate water. If you're looking for some beginning-level paddling in a rural valley with easy logistics, then this top section of the White offers a fine piece of water for paddling as well as for float-fishing.

Distance: 22.0 miles (shorter run possible)
Difficulty: Class I–II (beginner)
Craft: Canoes, kayaks
Approximate paddling time: 4 to 6 hours
Flows: 400 to 1,200 cfs
Season: May through June
Put-in: Bel Aire Wildlife Area at the confluence
Takeout: Meeker
Shuttle: Use County Road 8, which closely parallels the river, for both the put-in and takeout. The put-in is located at the confluence of the North and South Forks at the well-marked

Bel Aire State Wildlife Area, just below the hamlet of Buford.

To reach the takeout, head downstream on CR 8 into the town of Meeker. Look for signs for the White River Museum; turn left (south) off the main drag. Just upstream of the County Road 4 bridge is the museum; this is the takeout.

Additional information: The marked fishing access just upstream of the Sombrero Horse Camp can be used as a midpoint access point to shorten the length of this run.

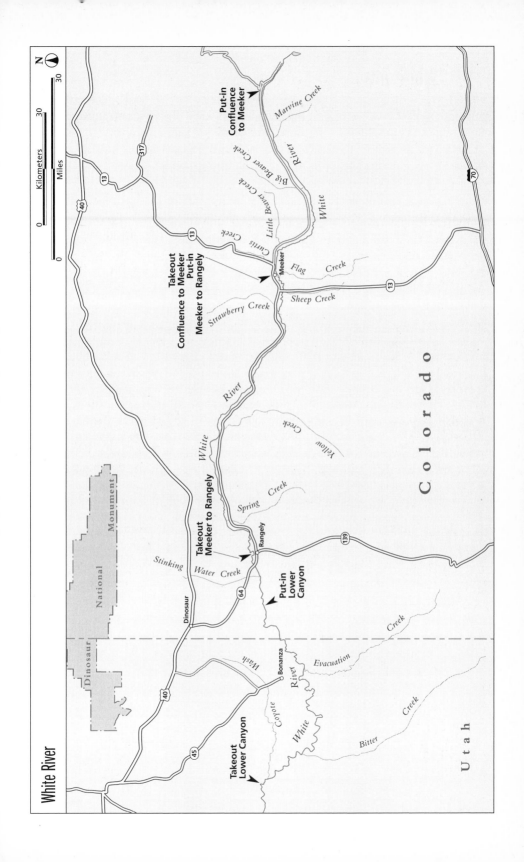

Meeker to Rangely

This section of the White is set in a quiet rural valley bottom lined with steep-sided buttes above. Much of the rock found in this area is oil shale, which is the target of the oil and gas companies seeking to extract low-grade oil-like material.

The river meanders and cruises downstream with relative ease and slight current throughout the length of this lazy section, offering fine open canoeing. About halfway through this section, Piceance Creek enters and noticeably increases the flow downstream, so the lifespan of the White is increased below this confluence. Just upstream of Rangely is Kenney Reservoir, which backs up the river for a few miles and requires a portage around Taylor Draw Dam. Below the dam, swift current carries paddlers down into Rangely.

Distance: 55.0 miles (shorter run possible)
Difficulty: Class I–II (beginner)
Craft: Canoes, kayaks
Approximate paddling time: Depends on the length of the run
Flows: 400 to 1,200 cfs
Season: May through June
Put-in: White River Museum, Meeker
Takeout: Highway 64 bridge on the west side of Rangely
Shuttle: Use Highway 64, which closely parallels the river, for both the put-in and takeout. To reach the put-in, in the town of Meeker, look for signs for the White River Museum. Turn to the south off the main drag. The museum is just upstream of the CR 4 bridge; this is the put-in.

To reach the takeout, head downstream (west) out of town, following signs for Highway 64. Coming into town, stay on Highway 64. As you leave the western end of town, Highway 64 crosses over the river; this is the takeout.

Additional information: Numerous access points can be used to shorten the overall length of a run. A popular put-in is located at Rio Blanco State Park downstream of Meeker. For another short paddle, use the put-in just below the dam at Tailrace picnic area and head down to Rangely.

Lower Canyon

This Lower Canyon of the White is a final surprise to paddlers as the rivers drops into a 600-foot-deep canyon. Not many paddlers know about this canyon, and it is quite a departure from the more open and rural sections upstream. Leaving behind much of the evidence of oil and gas exploitation, paddlers (primarily canoeists) ease into a nice lazy canyon float just west of Rangely.

Starting out with barren, dry hills, the White is an oasis in a bleak and hostile environment. As the river slides peacefully into the canyon, shale cliffs begin towering above the river; the narrow river bottom is choked with tamarisk as well as some cottonwoods and box elders. The river eases along. Higher water is preferable due to its steadier current, with nothing above small waves to deal with. In low water the river is much more of a flatwater slog but still scenic. In the last 12 miles or so above the confluence, the canyon walls step back and flatlands spread out over the Green River basin.

A view of the Lower White River as it slides into its Lower Canyon near the Colorado-Utah state line.

Distance: 60.0 miles (shorter run possible)
Difficulty: Class I–II (beginner)
Craft: Canoes, kayaks
Approximate paddling time: 3 to 4 days
Flows: 500 to 1,500 cfs
Season: May through June
Put-in: Rangely West Road
Takeout: River access just upstream of confluence (Utah)
Shuttle: To reach the put-in, head west from downtown Rangely on Highway 64. Shortly before the highway crosses the river, there is a gas station on the left (south) and a road. Turn left (south) onto Rangely West Road and follow it past the high school. Keep heading west approximately 10 miles to a Bureau of Land Management (BLM) river access point on the right; this is the put-in.

To reach the takeout, return to Highway 64 next to the gas station, turn left (west) and head toward Dinosaur. At the junction of Highway 64 and U.S. Highway 40, turn left (west) onto US 40 and follow it into Utah. Look for the County Road 45 turnoff to the south toward Bonanza. Follow this down to town, and then turn right (west) onto a dirt road that crosses Coyote Wash and eventually crosses the river; this is the takeout.

Additional information: An intermediate access point is located just south of Bonanza at the Utah CR 45 bridge. Head south from US 40; the access point is 25 river miles downstream of Rangely.

13 Colorado River

The headwater tributaries to the mighty Colorado River start high in the snow-capped peaks within Rocky Mountain National Park. Just outside the western border of the park, the outflow of Lake Granby marks the official start of the Colorado. The Colorado River cuts a relatively straight westward route through the state as it makes its descent toward the most famous section of river in the world farther downstream—the Grand Canyon.

Within the state borders, the Colorado River lazes its way through prime fishing waters near Hot Sulphur Springs and then suddenly tumbles downhill in a cold, swift torrent of expert-only whitewater through Gore Canyon. It then settles down throughout a rural valley in its upper sections, passing State Bridge, McCoy, and Dotsero.

The Colorado swallows up the Eagle River and makes another rush of expert whitewater through Barrel Springs, followed by the intermediate-friendly Shoshone Canyon. Downstream of this section, the river meanders and cruises along, paralleling Interstate 70 to the Colorado-Utah border. Just as the Colorado leaves the state, it enters the remote sandstone landscape of Ruby/Horsethief Canyon.

Middle Park Section

This irregularly paddled section of the Colorado River is known for its lazy drift-fishing and pleasant rural valley scenery. Please be very mindful of private property along both sides of the river throughout this stretch. Do not step ashore along this run, and use only designated access points. This is a benign and mild flatwater paddle. Steady current pushes paddlers downstream without any effort, and there are no rapids to speak of.

Distance: 9.0 miles
Difficulty: Class I (beginner)
Craft: Canoes, kayaks, rec boats, drift boats
Approximate paddling time: 3 to 4 hours
Flows: 400 to 1,500 cfs
Season: Year-round
Put-in: Sunset fishing access on south side of U.S. Highway 40
Takeout: Fishing access on east side of Highway 9 bridge
Shuttle: Head west out of Hot Sulphur Springs (elevation 7,655 feet) on US 40 and look for the well-marked Sunset fishing access sign; this is the put-in.

Continue heading west on US 40 into the town of Kremmling (elevation 7,411 feet), and then head south on Highway 9. Just south of town, Highway 9 crosses the river. Look for a fishing access sign on the east side of the road; this is the take out.

Additional information: Be sure to take out here—shortly downstream, the Colorado drops into expert-only Gore Canyon (Class V).

Pumphouse Section

This is perhaps the most popular section of river in Colorado. Summer weekends can be a crazy zoo of all types of craft at the put-in and takeout. Paddlers will find a nice section of mildly challenging whitewater, a remote-feeling canyon, easy shuttle logistics, and year-round water.

Paddlers start out with a short valley float before entering Little Gore Canyon, where Needle Eye Rapid (Class II+), the crux rapid of the run, is found in the middle of the canyon. At high water, good waves form within the canyon.

All too soon, the canyon opens up and a bridge crosses over the river at Radium Recreation site; this can be used as an access point. Below this bridge, the river again bends away from the road and cuts into Red Gorge, which contains numerous Class II rapids. Below this canyon, rural paddling and gentle waves bring paddlers down to the takeout.

Distance: 11.0 miles
Difficulty: Class II–II+ (advanced beginner/ intermediate)
Craft: Canoes, kayaks, rafts
Approximate paddling time: 3 to 5 hours
Flows: 500 to 2,000 cfs
Season: Year-round
Put-in: Pumphouse Recreation Site off County Road 1

Takeout: Rancho del Rio or Yarmony Bridge just downstream
Shuttle: All access is off CR 1, which is located off Highway 9 just south of the town of Kremmling. All access points are well marked.
Additional information: Radium Recreation Site (off County Road 11) can be used as an intermediate access point to shorten this run.

State Bridge Section

This short section of river offers a roadside sampling of pleasant beginner/intermediate river running. Nice eddies, smaller waves, and nice scenery offer a short but sweet section for budding paddlers or those seeking "one more run" before dark. This short piece of river is often added to the upstream run or used as a bit higher put-in for a lower run.

Distance: 3.0 miles
Difficulty: Class II (beginner/intermediate)
Craft: Canoes, kayaks, rafts
Approximate paddling time: 1 to 2 hours
Flows: 500 to 2,000 cfs
Season: Year-round
Put-in: Rancho del Rio or Yarmony Bridge
Takeout: State Bridge; parking area on river-left off the east side of Highway 131
Shuttle: Using CR 1 as the main route, Rancho

del Rio is a fee access area for a put-in. Just downstream, the Yarmony Bridge is a free alternative put-in point.

Head downstream to the historic area known as State Bridge, where CR 1 meets with Highway 131. Turn left onto Highway 131, cross over the river, and look for an immediate left turn into a dirt pullout. The takeout is on river-left, just upstream of the bridge.

Colorado River

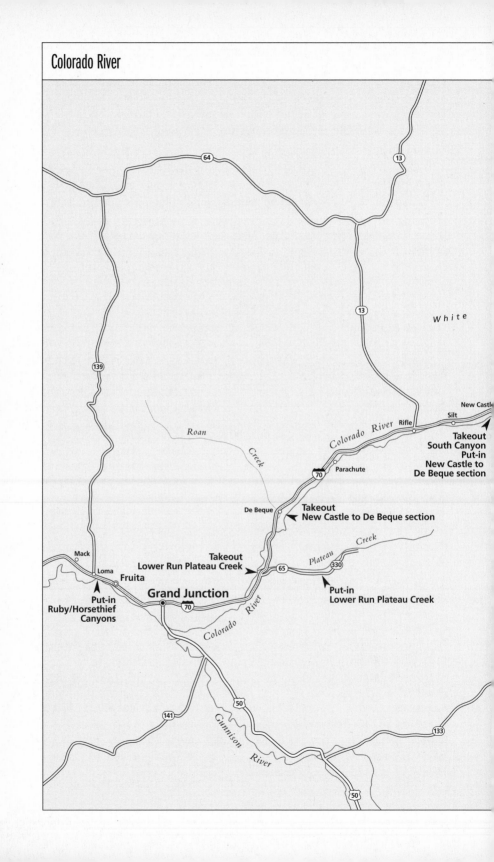

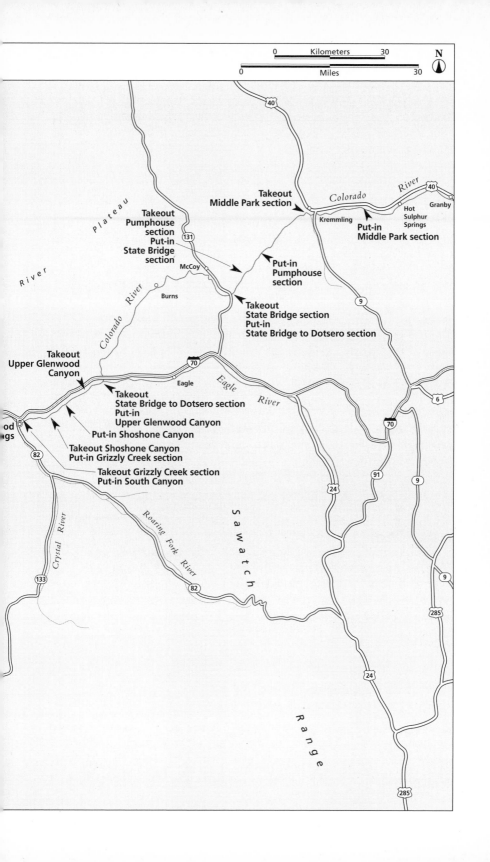

State Bridge to Dotsero Section

A rural road parallels this section of the Upper Colorado, making shorter runs easily possible. You can also scout the majority of the river while making the shuttle. This section is a rural, lazy paddle interspersed with fun Class II rapids between flat sections of moving current.

This zone is great for open canoeists and family raft trips, as well as beginning kayakers. The largest rapid on this section—Rodeo Rapid (Class III)—is located just downstream of the little town of Bond. Be wary of multiple bridge abutments along this entire section; these can pose serious hazards in higher water.

Distance: 45.0 miles (shorter runs are possible)

Difficulty: Class II–II+ (beginner/intermediate)

Craft: Canoes, kayaks, rafts

Approximate paddling time: Varies based on length of run

Flows: 500 to 2,000 cfs

Season: Year-round; best flows May through July

Put-in: Highway 131, State Bridge

Takeout: Dotsero boat ramp at the confluence of the Colorado and Eagle Rivers

Shuttle: Head north from the put-in on Highway 131. After the town of McCoy, look for signs for County Road 301. Turn left (west) onto this dirt road and follow it alongside the river. This road, also known as Colorado River Road, can be used for the shuttle from this point on. Intermediate access points include Catamount Bridge Recreation Site, Burns and Pinball river access sites, and Cottonwood Island Recreation Site.

The lowest takeout is located at the Dotsero boat ramp, just on the south side of I-70 at the confluence of the Colorado and Eagle Rivers.

Additional information: Check out other beginner/intermediate paddling options just upstream on the Eagle River (see the Eagle River section).

Upper Glenwood Canyon

This section of the Colorado parallels the busy four-lane I-70, and the paddling is easy once you're on the water. With the combination of traffic and flatwater, why would anyone want to paddle this section of river? It's because this is the dramatic entrance into Glenwood Canyon. The run starts slow and open in a rural valley before being squeezed between narrow canyon walls that tower more than 3,000 feet at its deepest point. On the lower portion of this section, you'll be paddling the backwaters of Shoshone Reservoir (built in 1909). If you're looking for an easily accessed, albeit noisy, flatwater paddle to break up the drive, then this might be just what you need.

Distance: 8.0 miles
Difficulty: Class I (beginner)
Craft: Canoes, kayaks, rec boats
Approximate paddling time: 2 to 4 hours
Flows: 500 to 3,000 cfs
Season: Year-round
Put-in: Dotsero boat ramp, at the confluence of the Colorado and Eagle Rivers

Takeout: Hanging Lake Trailhead
Shuttle: Use I-70 for both the put-in and takeout. To reach the put-in, take exit 133 and head the south.

To reach the takeout, return to I-70 and head west to exit 125. Use the Shoshone Power Plant boat ramp as the takeout.

Shoshone Canyon

Short but sweet whitewater, Shoshone is the most-used, year-round, intermediate section of river in the state. This run combines the ideal factors of reliable water, easy access, good rapids, and a variety of play spots that have paddlers smiling at the takeout.

All the rapids can be seen from the river-right river trail for scouting the run, and numerous eddies can be caught to break apart each rapid. The rapids of note in downstream order are the Wall, Bonehead, Tombstone, and Superstition. Hard-core paddlers play this section hard for longer runs or do numerous runs to satisfy their adrenaline thirst.

Distance: 1.5 miles
Difficulty: Class III (intermediate)
Craft: Whitewater kayaks, canoes, rafts
Approximate paddling time: 0.5 to 2 hours
Flows: 500 to 3,000 cfs
Season: Year-round
Put-in: Exit 123 off I-70 east

Takeout: Exit 121 off I-70 West (Grizzly Creek boat ramp)
Shuttle: From the town of Glenwood Springs, head east on I-70 to the takeout at Grizzly Creek (exit 121). Leave a vehicle at the takeout, or follow the river trail upstream.

The put-in (exit 123) allows only westward entry back onto I-70.

Grizzly Creek Section

This section is often paddled as a "cool-down" for the Shoshone section just upstream or as a learning section for budding whitewater paddlers. The Grizzly Creek run marks the end of Glenwood Canyon's steep-walled scenery as the Colorado River flows into the town of Glenwood Springs.

Numerous straightforward rapids mark the first half of the trip down to No Name (exit 119); the second half of the trip eases down into town. Year-round water offers a reliable section for paddlers to get out and work on their skills.

*A kayaking class enjoys a sunny afternoon paddle down into
Glenwood Springs on the Grizzly Creek section.*
COURTESY OF RENAISSANCE GUIDES

Distance: 6.0 miles
Difficulty: Class II–II+ (advanced beginner/intermediate)
Craft: Whitewater kayaks/canoes, rafts
Approximate paddling time: 2 to 3 hours
Flows: 500 to 3,000 cfs
Season: Year-round
Put-in: Exit 121 off I-70 (Grizzly Creek boat ramp)
Takeout: Two Rivers Park in Glenwood Springs, exit 116 off I-70

Shuttle: Use I-70 for the put-in and takeout. To reach the put-in, take exit 121 to the Grizzly Creek boat ramp.

To reach the takeout, head west on I-70 into Glenwood Springs and get off at exit 116. Turn right off the exit ramp and drive to a traffic light. Turn left at the light onto U.S. Highway 6. Head downstream less than a mile, looking for signs for Two Rivers Park (restrooms and park facilities); this is the takeout.

South Canyon

If you're looking for a bit more paddling in the Glenwood area, the South Canyon section offers another piece of quality paddling on the Colorado River just west of Glenwood Springs. As they leave the put-in, paddlers will find swift current and gentle wave trains that carry them downstream to the major whitewater of this section—South Canyon Rapid (Class II–II+). This rapid is located near Mile 5 of the trip, just upstream of a bridge accessed off I-70 (exit 111). This rapid also forms a great eddy-accessed surf wave when the flow is around 2,000 cfs. Below this point, the river clips along with good eddylines and smaller waves to the takeout at the town of New Castle.

Distance: 11.0 miles
Difficulty: Class II–II+ (advanced beginner/intermediate)
Craft: Whitewater kayaks/canoes, rafts
Approximate paddling time: 2 or 4 hours
Flows: 500 to 3,500 cfs
Season: Year-round
Put-in: Two Rivers Park (restrooms and park facilities), just downstream on Frontage Road off I-70 exit 116
Takeout: Tibbett's pullout on river-left, off I-70 exit 105
Shuttle: Use I-70 to access both the put-in and takeout. To reach the put-in, head west and take exit 116 to Glenwood Springs. Turn right off the exit ramp and drive to a traffic light. Turn left onto US 6. Head downstream less than a mile, looking for signs for Two Rivers Park; this is the put-in.

To reach the takeout, head west on I-70 to exit 105. Make a U-turn and head back upstream 2 miles to a large dirt pullout east of New Castle that is only accessible from I-70 west. This is known as Tibbett's and is the takeout.
Additional information: Instead of paddling this section, you can park and play at South Canyon Wave and also park and play at the newly built (2008) play wave on the west end of town.

New Castle to De Beque Section

This long section of the Colorado is included in this guide more for its continuation and interest to paddlers than for its actual popularity as a paddling destination. Largely because of the busy-ness of this section—it's closely paralleled by I-70, a railroad, and a frontage road—and its mild flatwater nature, wilderness lovers and whitewater seekers tend to drive right past these miles of river.

Here the Colorado floats through a wide rural valley that offers a broad meandering channel braided around islands covered with groves of cottonwoods, willows, and box elders. Countless Canada geese, ducks, and other waterfowl can be spied along this section of river. Near the bottom end of the run the Colorado drops into De Beque Canyon, which features narrow sandstone walls. The current speeds up in the canyon, but there are no real rapids, just good current and occasional waves. Be extremely careful navigating past several diversion head gates on this section. In addition, multiple dams must be portaged on the lower end of the run below Beavertail Mountain, shortly upstream of the lowest possible takeout in the town of De Beque.

Distance: 64.0 miles (shorter runs possible)
Difficulty: Class I–II (beginner)
Craft: Canoes, kayaks, rafts
Approximate paddling time: Varies based on length of run
Flows: 1,000 to 5,000 cfs
Season: Year-round
Put-in: Tibbett's pullout on river-left, off I-70 exit 105
Takeout: De Beque, off I-70 exit 62
Shuttle: Use I-70 to access both the put-in and takeout. To reach the put-in, head west on I-70 to exit 105. Make a U-turn and head back upstream 2 miles to a large dirt pullout called Tibbett's; this is the put-in.
To reach the takeout, take exit 62 off I-70

and exit right (north) on County Road 204. This road will cross the river and a river access point can be found next to the north side of the bridge.
Additional information: A recommended day trip is to put in at New Castle and take out in Rifle (I-70 exit 90). This offers a 15-mile Class I paddle with relative seclusion in spite of the nearby interstate. For paddlers wishing to extend the run, the river remains straightforward in difficulty, but care must be taken around man-made diversions and portaging dams farther downstream. To avoid the dams, use a lower takeout point near Beavertail Mountain, just upstream of Plateau Creek.

Ruby/Horsethief Canyons

Ruby/Horsethief is the first-ever overnight river trip for many regional paddlers. In fact, this trip is often the first-ever paddling experience for the next generation of young paddlers—it is a great family float trip. This is not a dramatic steep-walled raging river canyon; it's more of a gentle float beneath sandstone cliff walls, with nice and open sagebrush-filled camping.

Beginner paddlers will have little stress on this trip. A wide-open river channel is punctuated with swift, steady current, nice eddies, and occasional waves at certain water levels. Desert enthusiasts will find good hiking up the side canyons of Rattlesnake (near Mile 3.5) and Mee (near Mile 14) Canyons.

The most popular overnight site is in the Black Rocks area (near Mile 16). The Blacks Rocks area marks the most significant swirly water and smaller waves.

Distance: 25.0 miles
Difficulty: Class I–II- (beginner)
Craft: Kayaks, canoes, rafts, rec boats
Approximate paddling time: 2 to 3 days
Flows: 1,500 to 10,000 cfs
Season: Year-round

Put-in: I-70 exit 15 (Loma boat ramp)
Takeout: Westwater Canyon launch site (Utah)
Shuttle: To reach the put-in, head west on I-70 out of the city of Grand Junction to exit 15 (Loma). Head south off the exit ramp and follow a short road to the put-in beach.

Ruby/Horsethief is often the site for weekend river flotillas.
COURTESY OF RENAISSANCE GUIDES

To reach the takeout, get back on I-70, heading west into Utah. Take exit 225 (Westwater) and head southwest to the launch area. **Additional information:** Ruby/Horsethief does not require a permit and is often paddled as a warm-up or add-on to the permit-required Westwater Canyon (Class III–IV) section just downstream.

Plateau Creek

One of the largest drainages off the flat-topped Grand Mesa, Plateau Creek is a little gem of a creek when it is flowing. Entirely free-flowing and springing to life during snowmelt, Plateau Creek flows fast and continuously downhill due west until it drops into the Colorado River just upstream of Grand Junction. The Plateau Creek Valley is a nice tucked-away area of relative tranquility set beneath dry sandstone-cliff walls.

Lower Run Plateau Creek

This bottom section of Plateau Creek—where the creek drops steadily into a sandstone canyon—is where the intermediate paddling lies. Constant flow carries paddlers downstream before the last mile or so of the run offers up the more challenging whitewater. Below the highway bridge on the last portion of this run, the action really heats up. The whitewater climbs to good Class III, with the narrow, steeper channel presenting a risk of strainers and wood debris. Scout as best as possible while running shuttle, and put in for a good little intermediate creek run to break up the drive along I-70.

Distance: 8.0 miles (shorter run possible)
Difficulty: Class III (intermediate)
Craft: Canoes, kayaks
Approximate paddling time: 2 to 3 hours
Flows: 300 to 800 cfs
Season: April through June
Put-in: Mile Marker 53 on Highway 65

Takeout: Canyon mouth on Highway 65 at Mile Marker 49 on I-70
Shuttle: Use Highway 65 as the primary access route for this section. Both the put-in and takeout are well marked and easy to find. To reach Highway 65, take exit 49 off I-70 and head east towards the town of Collbran.

---

14 Blue River

The swift-flowing Blue River flows out of Dillon Reservoir in the heart of Summit County. Fed from high-mountain tributaries flowing off numerous adjacent ski areas (Breckenridge, Keystone, Arapaho Basin, and Copper Mountain), the Blue fills up Dillon Reservoir and then flows downstream, making a swift journey northward before joining the Colorado River. Its rocky course is punctuated by the erratic releases from Dillon and Green Mountain Dams. The dams release water from the bottom of their reservoirs, thus offering coldwater paddling.

Upper Blue River

This section of the Upper Blue contains the best whitewater in a short but sweet section of Class II–III intermediate whitewater. With Highway 9 paralleling most of the river for easy access, the Blue drops down away from the road to offer a more secluded, heavily wooded canyon.

Down here paddlers will encounter the crux whitewater of the run at Boulder Creek Rapid, which is marked by Boulder Creek tumbling into the river on river-left. Paddlers who don't notice the creek come upon the rapid unexpectedly on a relatively blind corner. Below this rapid, more continuous Class II–III whitewater carries paddlers swiftly out of the canyon toward the takeout back out by the highway.

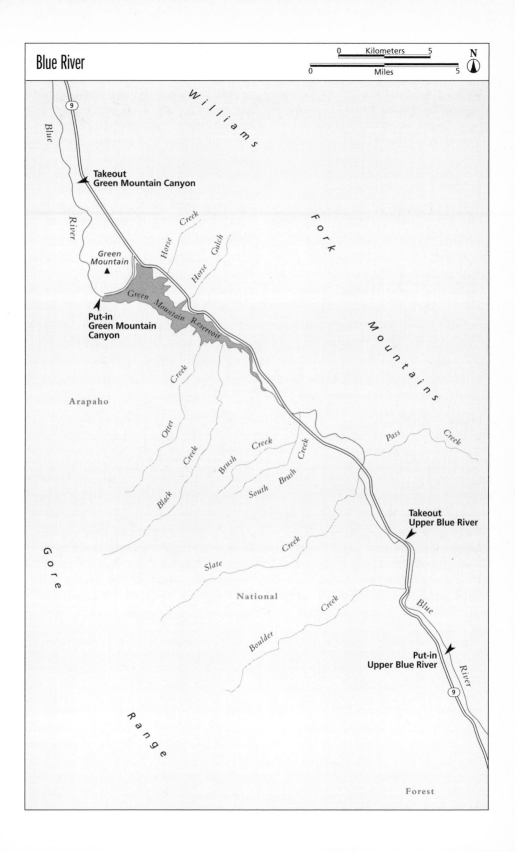

Blue River

Kilometers 5

Miles 5

N

Blue River

9

Williams

Fork

Mountains

Takeout
Green Mountain Canyon

Horse *Creek*

Horse *Gulch*

Green
Mountain
▲

Green Mountain Reservoir

Put-in
Green Mountain
Canyon

Creek

Arapaho

Otter

Creek

Black

Creek

Brush *Creek*

South Brush *Creek*

Pass *Creek*

Takeout
Upper Blue River

Creek

Gore

Slate

National

Creek

Blue

Put-in
Upper Blue River

River

9

Range

Boulder

Forest

Distance: 3.0 miles
Difficulty: Class II–III (intermediate)
Craft: Canoes, kayaks, rafts
Approximate paddling time: 1 to 3 hours
Flows: Recommended flows 300 to 1,000 cfs
Season: Dam controlled; mid-May through late June
Put-in: Quaking Creek Ranch
Takeout: Columbine Landing
Shuttle: To reach the put-in, head north 8 miles from the town of Silverthorne on Highway 9. The put-in is near Mile Marker 108.

To reach the takeout, continue north on Highway 9 past Blue River Campground to the well-marked Columbine Landing takeout/access point.

Additional information: Another possible paddle is from the town of Silverthorne to the put-in of this run (9.0 miles, Class I–II), with access along Highway 9. Or put in at the Columbine Landing and continue down into Green Mountain Reservoir (8.0 miles, Class I–II), with a takeout at the Blue River fishing access point off Highway 9.

Green Mountain Canyon

Putting in just below Green Mountain Dam, paddlers immediately drop into a nice, secluded river canyon. The steep hillsides are lined with pines and fir, and the chilly water speeds along at a steady pace with tight eddies, wave trains, and a few Class II–III rapids. This is a nice intermediate run for paddlers working on skills, as well as those looking for the seclusion of a pleasant river canyon.

Distance: 4.0 miles
Difficulty: Class II–III (intermediate)
Craft: Canoes, kayaks, rafts
Approximate paddling time: 1 to 3 hours
Flows: Dam controlled; flows greater than 300 to 1,000 cfs recommended
Season: Late-summer/early-fall dam releases
Put-in: Below Green Mountain Dam
Takeout: Spring Creek Bridge on 10 Road
Shuttle: To reach the put-in, just north of Green Mountain Reservoir off Highway 9, turn west on Heeney Road and drive on top of the dam. The put-in is just across the dam on river-left.

To reach the takeout, return to Highway 9 and head north to Spring Creek Road (10 Road). Turn west and take out at the bridge over the river.

Additional information: Below this takeout, the Blue River lazes 9 miles northward to its confluence with the Colorado River. This beginner section contains gentle current flowing past private ranches and farmland. Put-in is at the Spring Creek Bridge. To reach the takeout, head north on Highway 9 to County Road 1 (Trough Road) and head west. Just before crossing the Blue River, turn north on County Road 21 and use the fishing access at the confluence as a takeout.

15 Eagle River

The Eagle is a swift, free-flowing tributary to the Colorado River. Flowing westward out of Vail Valley with Interstate 70 and U.S. Highway 6 paralleling its course, the Eagle is a lively river with fine intermediate paddling sections, but it is not a wilderness run by any means. The Eagle River is a welcome retreat from the land of high-speed interstates and conspicuous wealth that fill the valley. Busy and action packed near the top and lazy near the bottom, the Eagle has a section for both beginner and intermediate paddlers.

Upper Eagle

The Upper Eagle is a fast-paced, nearly continuous section of intermediate whitewater that flows past fir trees and a heavily vegetated shallow canyon.

Putting in just below the short but very rowdy Dowd's Chutes (Class IV), the Upper Eagle tumbles downstream through a busy maze of more continuous Class III rapids. At higher flows, the eddies fly by and paddlers get a face full of water as they crash through numerous waves. As the water level drops a bit more, rocks poke out for good maneuvering, and eddies become more inviting.

Distance: 7.0 miles
Difficulty: Class III (Intermediate)
Craft: Whitewater kayaks, rafts
Approximate paddling time: 2 to 3 hours
Flows: 500 to 2,500 cfs
Season: High-water runoff May through June; lower water levels into July and August
Put-in: Riverbend bus stop off US 6
Takeout: Water treatment plant downstream of the town of Edwards
Shuttle: The fastest route for shuttling on this run is I-70. The put-in is located off exit 171. Head downstream about 2 miles to the Riverbend Condos; use a small set of steps to reach the river.

To reach the takeout, get back on I-70 and head west to the town of Edwards (exit 163). Head south from the exit off I-70 to a junction with US 6. Turn right (west) on US 6 and travel 1 mile from the lights to the next bridge over the river. Park on the north side of the river near the water treatment plant.

Additional information: A parking lot on the southwest side of the Hurd Lane bridge in the town of Avon (I-70 exit 167) can be used as a midway access point. A surf wave can be found underneath the upstream side of the bridge. The Eagle slows down and gets slightly easier below this access point.

Lower Eagle

This section of the Eagle is the most popular for commercial raft trips and paddlers. A step down in difficulty from the upstream run, this section offers a majority of Class II rapids, with a few very manageable Class III rapids thrown in. Larger rapids of note on this run include Trestle Bridge, Interstate, and Dead Cow Rapids. In all,

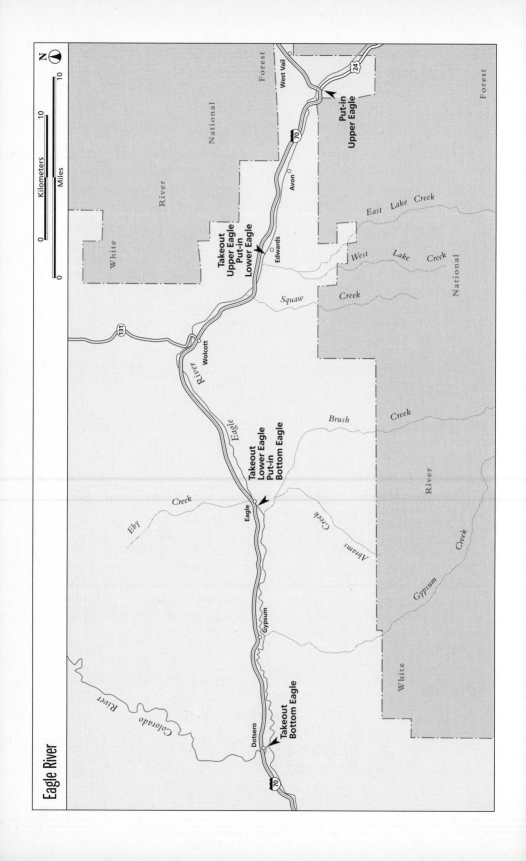

Eagle River

this popular section of the Eagle offers a quality paddling experience as the river tumbles its way out of the mountains and into sandstone plateaus characteristic of the Western Slope.

Distance: 18.0 miles
Difficulty: Class II–III (advanced beginner/ intermediate)
Craft: Whitewater kayaks/canoes, rafts
Approximate paddling time: 3 to 5 hours
Flows: 600 to 3,000 cfs
Season: Free flowing, with high-water runoff May through June; lower water levels into July and August
Put-in: Water treatment plant 1 mile downstream of the town of Edwards
Takeout: Chambers Park, next to the fairgrounds in the town of Eagle

Shuttle: The best roadside scouting along the shuttle can be had by using US 6, which closely parallels the river. Those looking for a more high-speed shuttle can jump back onto I-70 and use the Eagle exit (exit 147) for the takeout. The actual takeout is Chambers Park, near the fairgrounds on the west side of the town of Eagle.
Additional information: The BLM access located 0.5 mile downstream of Wolcott (I-70 exit 157) can be used as a midway access point.

Bottom Eagle

Looking for a slightly mellower run on the Eagle for beginners or a family float? Then the Bottom Eagle is for you. Down here the Eagle slows and mellows from its upriver rapid and rocky descent and wanders a bit more through farmland and past cottonwood trees before being swallowed up by the Colorado River.

Distance: 15.0 miles
Difficulty: Class I–II (beginner to intermediate)
Craft: Kayaks, canoes, rec boats, rafts
Approximate paddling time: 3 to 5 hours
Flows: 600 to 3,000 cfs
Season: Free flowing, with high-water runoff May through June; lower water levels into July and August
Put-in: Chambers Park, next to the fairgrounds on the west side of the town of Eagle
Takeout: Dotsero boat launch/access point off I-70 exit 133

Shuttle: Put in near the fairgrounds in the town of Eagle (I-70 exit 147).

To reach the takeout, continue west on I-70 to Dotsero (exit 133). Look for signs for the fishing access to the south of the interstate.
Additional information: A midway access point off the County Road 101 bridge (I-70 exit 140) in the town Gypsum can be used to shorten this section. The run from Eagle to Gypsum provides swifter current and paddling. Gypsum to Dotsero is a slower, gentler paddle.

16 Roaring Fork River

Tumbling off the western side of the Sawatch Mountain Range and Independence Pass through the famously ritzy mountain town of Aspen, the free-flowing Roaring Fork races 60 miles northward to its confluence with the Colorado River in the town of Glenwood Springs. Numerous quality paddling sections, good access, and a nice river valley setting combine to make the Roaring Fork River a sought-after destination for intermediate paddlers.

Upper Woody Creek Section

This section of the Roaring Fork churns downstream on a steady, continuous course through Class II–III whitewater. Because of its continuous nature, this is strong intermediate territory more for its fast pace than for its technical difficulty or individual rapids.

Length: 4.0 miles
Difficulty: Class III (intermediate)
Craft: Canoes, kayaks, rafts
Approximate paddling time: 1 to 2 hours
Flows: 500 to 1,700 cfs
Season: May through July
Put-in: Upper Woody Creek Bridge, located at Mile Marker 34.5 on Highway 82
Takeout: Lower Woody Creek Bridge, located at Mile Marker 31 on Highway 82

Shuttle: Quick and easy shuttles are done on Highway 82, which offers glimpses of the river for en-route scouting.
Additional information: Just upstream of the town of Aspen is a beginner section (5.0 miles, Class I) that flows through a pleasant meadow. Just below Aspen is a well-known advanced section known as the Slaughterhouse Run (Class IV).

Toothache Section

This quick blast-downstream run is also known as the Lower Woody Creek Run. The name Toothache comes from the largest rapid on this run—Toothache Rapid (Class III). This section of river flows into Woody Creek Canyon, and a series of Class III wave trains fill the heart of the run. Toothache is the largest of the straightforward waves.

Distance: 6.0 miles
Difficulty: Class III (intermediate)
Craft: Canoes, kayaks, rafts

Approximate paddling time: 2 to 3 hours
Flows: 500 to 1,700 cfs
Season: May through July

◀ *Rafters pass by numerous golf courses, typical of the middle section of the Eagle River.*

Roaring Fork River

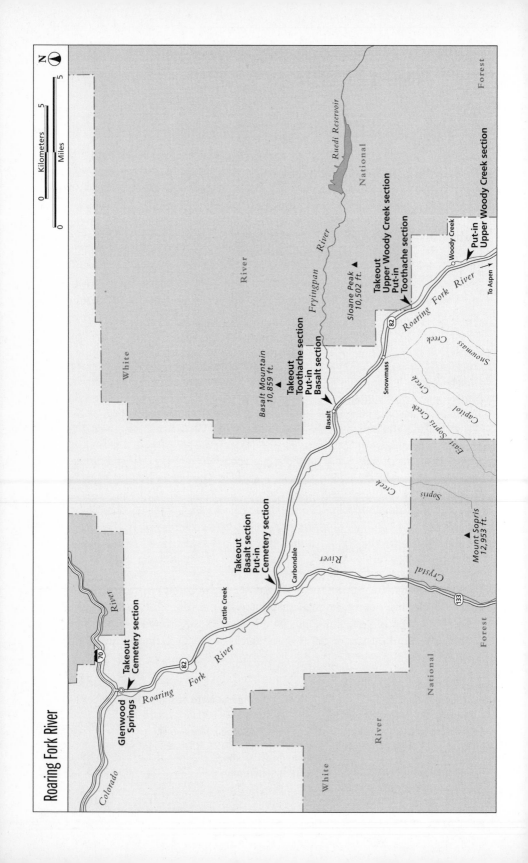

Put-in: Lower Woody Creek Bridge, located at Mile Marker 31 on Highway 82

Takeout: Highway 82 bridge at Mile Marker 25

Shuttle: Quick and easy shuttles are done on Highway 82, which also offers glimpses of the river for en-route scouting.

Basalt Section

This section of the Roaring Fork is a noticeable step down in difficulty from the upstream runs. It's characterized by swift, steady current; a meandering gravel bar; and braided channels. This is a pleasant run for those seeking Class II whitewater at most (found just below the second bridge on the run).

Distance: 12.0 miles

Difficulty: Class I-II (beginner/intermediate)

Craft: Canoes, kayaks, rafts

Approximate paddling time: 2 to 4 hours

Flows: 500 to 2,000 cfs

Season: May through July

Put-in: 7-11 parking lot in the town of Basalt, next to the confluence with the Fryingpan River

Takeout: Highway 133 bridge in Carbondale

Shuttle: Quick and easy shuttles are done on Highway 82, which also offers glimpses of the river for en-route scouting.

Cemetery Section

Set beneath the beautiful Mount Sopris, this lowest section of the Roaring Fork typically has larger flows. The put-in is located just above the confluence with the Crystal River, and this section has a longer paddling season that other upstream runs.

The gradient drops down as the river flows through private ranches and open farmland on both sides of the river. As it approaches its confluence with the Colorado, the Roaring Fork makes a final flexing of its whitewater muscles at Cemetery Rapid—0.25 mile of Class II-II+ whitewater. Below this rapid, paddlers enter the backstreets of Glenwood Springs.

Distance: 12.0 miles

Difficulty: Class II-II+ (advanced beginner/ intermediate)

Craft: Canoes, kayaks, rafts

Approximate paddling time: 3 to 4 hours

Flows: 500 to 2,500 cfs

Season: April through August

Put-in: Highway 133 bridge in Carbondale

Takeout: Veltus Park in Glenwood Springs

Shuttle: To reach the put-in, turn south onto Highway 133 from Highway 82, heading into Carbondale. The bridge immediately across the river is the put-in.

To reach the takeout, take Highway 82 into Glenwood Springs. Once in town, Highway 82 becomes Grand Avenue. Turn west onto Eighth Street, cross the river, and then turn left (south) and drive for 1 block to Veltus Park.

Additional information: A midway access point can be used at the Iron Bridge (at the 6.0-mile point of the run), just below Highway 82. Down to this bridge is excellent beginner paddling (Class I-II). A possible downstream takeout is located below the confluence with the Colorado River at Two Rivers Park on river-right.

17 Crystal River

The Crystal tumbles out of the West Elks Mountains hard and fast and, yes, crystal clear. The headwater gorges of the Crystal form some of the most committing and expert-only gorges in the whole state. The mid-reaches of the Crystal create a technical onslaught of challenging advanced/expert-level whitewater.

It is in the lower reaches that intermediate paddlers will find fitting sections for paddling the Crystal. Flowing northward around the western flank of beautiful Mount Sopris, the Crystal is paralleled by windy Highway 133, which offers mostly unobstructed views of the riverbed and the majority of the rapids through this pristine river canyon.

Avalanche Section

This section is the first easier section from the tumultuous upstream runs, while still offering a canyonlike setting. This nice roadside run begins with swift and semicontinuous Class II whitewater. About midway through this run, the largest rapid—the Big One (Cass III)—is encountered as a narrow chute with large straightforward waves. This run loses its eddies at high water, and the swift, cold water requires extra caution.

Distance: 5.0 miles
Difficulty: Class III (intermediate)
Craft: Whitewater kayaks
Approximate paddling time: 1 to 2 hours
Flows: 300 to 700 cfs
Season: May through early July
Put-in: Avalanche Creek pullout off Highway 133 near Mile Marker 57
Takeout: BRB Campground just off Highway 133 near Mile Marker 62

Shuttle: Highway 133 provides a quick, easy shuttle as well as scouting opportunities while shuttling.

Additional information: Continue farther upstream along Highways 133 for roadside scouting of the advanced/expert runs of the Upper Crystal.

Lower Section

As the Crystal flows out of its narrow river canyon, it offers up its easiest section of paddling, from the canyon mouth down to the confluence with the Roaring Fork River next to Carbondale. The river meanders with steady current through open pastureland and past ranches. Care is needed passing underneath numerous bridges, as well as with high water that forms eddyless action.

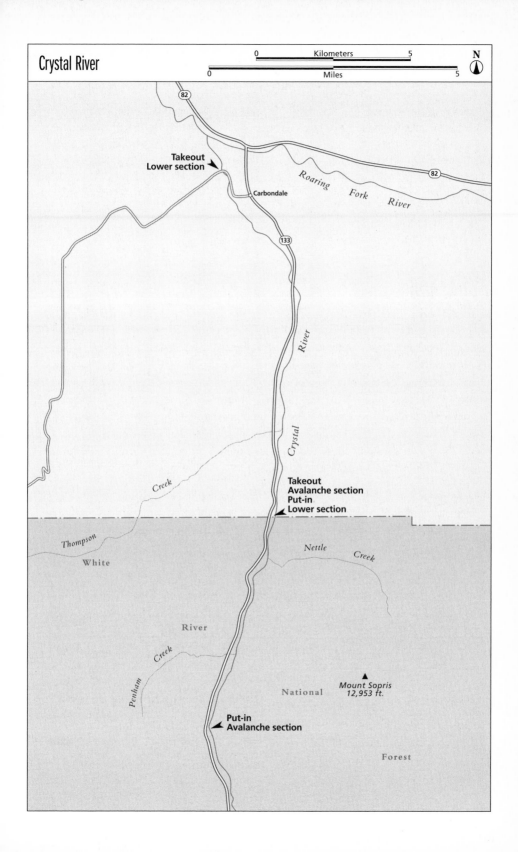

Distance: 6.0 miles
Difficulty: Class II (advanced beginner/intermediate)
Craft: Whitewater kayaks
Approximate paddling time: 2 to 3 hours
Flows: 300 to 700 cfs
Season: May through early July
Put-in: BRB Campground just off Highway 133 near Mile Marker 62
Takeout: Bridge over the Crystal River next to Colorado Rocky Mountain School

Shuttle: Highway 133 provides a quick, easy shuttle as well as scouting opportunities while shuttling.
Additional information: Continue farther upstream along Highway 133 for roadside scouting of the advanced/expert runs of the Upper Crystal. While in the area, check out other beginner/intermediate runs on the Roaring Fork River upstream and downstream of Carbondale.

18 Taylor River

The Taylor is a semi-secluded special little river. Its nice canyon, busy but forgiving whitewater, easy access, and abundant camping provide a rewarding paddling experience for advanced beginner to intermediate paddlers.

Dam controlled and flowing out of Taylor Park Reservoir, the Taylor begins its southwestern route toward the East River by dropping through a pleasant pine and fir forested canyon while dancing around numerous granite boulders and rocks. The overall nature of the Taylor is of a swift-flowing technical river for paddling that is fairly straightforward and forgiving. A rural Forest Service road parallels the entire river to allow for easy access and scouting.

Taylor Canyon

This upper section of the Taylor is considered to be the uppermost intermediate run below the upstream reservoir. The Taylor Canyon section drops through a narrow and pretty roadside canyon. The upper portion of the run offers more challenging whitewater with a section of large boulders known as the Slot (Class III). Just below here, some surf waves appear at certain levels.

Stay heads up for the downstream rapids of Toilet Bowl and Tombstone (both Class III). Because of its dam-controlled releases, shady canyon, and slightly higher elevation, water temperatures on this section can be quite chilly, even in summer.

Distance: 5.0 miles
Difficulty: Class II-III (intermediate)
Craft: Canoes, kayaks, rafts
Approximate paddling time: 2 to 3 hours
Flows: 300 to 800 cfs
Season: Dam controlled; May through July

Put-in: Forest Service New Generation put-in
Takeout: South Bank launch/access point just upstream of Spring Creek
Shuttle: For an easy, quick shuttle and scouting opportunities while shuttling, use Forest Service Road 745.

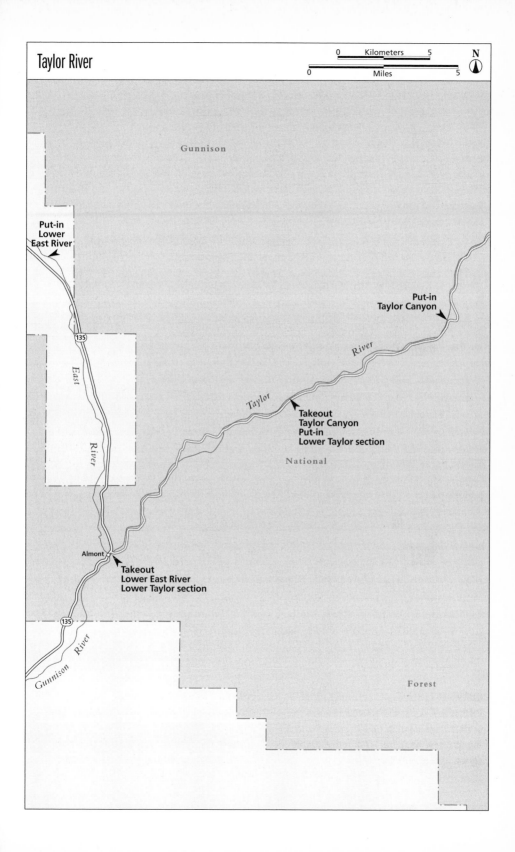

Taylor River

0 — Kilometers — 5
0 — Miles — 5

N

Gunnison

Put-in
Lower
East River

Put-in
Taylor Canyon

135

East

River

Taylor

River

Takeout
Taylor Canyon
Put-in
Lower Taylor section

National

Almont

Takeout
Lower East River
Lower Taylor section

135

Gunnison River

Gunnison River

Forest

Lower Taylor Section

This lower section of Taylor offers easier paddling, as the river begins settling down as it exits its upstream canyon. Still cold and swift water flows into mostly Class II wave-filled whitewater, and the canyon walls open up as the river passes through an open valley just below the put-in. Easy roadside access and easier rapids make this section a great learning section set in a pleasant valley.

Distance: 7.5 miles
Difficulty: Class I-II- (beginner/intermediate)
Craft: Canoes, kayaks, rafts
Approximate paddling time: 2 to 3 hours
Flows: 300 to 800 cfs
Season: Dam controlled; May through July
Put-in: South Bank launch/access point
Takeout: Confluence access point, just below the East River off Highway 135
Shuttle: For an easy, quick shuttle and scouting opportunities while shuttling, use FSR 745 to reach the put-in.

To reach the takeout, head downriver on FSR 745 to the junction with Highway 135 and turn left (south) onto Highway 135. Go a short distance and cross the bridge over the East River. Pull into the parking lot on the east side of the highway at the confluence of the East and the Taylor Rivers.

East River

Draining the upstream valley around the town of Crested Butte, the East River is formed through the confluence of multiple, small, waterfall-filled creeks upstream. Entirely free flowing and formed of snowmelt, the East River flows strong in high water as a continuous stream of current down to its confluence with the Taylor River. It is only in the lower section of the river that beginners will find an appropriate section for paddling on the East.

Lower Section

Down here near the bottom of the East River, the river flows widely through a spacious open valley around ranches and farms. This section of river contains a shallow sandy river bottom with no rocks impeding its course, so the paddling is a straightforward and steady downstream current run. Use caution at the highest water levels because of washed-out eddies. Otherwise the Lower East River provides another nice afternoon of paddling in the area.

Distance: 11.0 miles
Difficulty: Class I-II (beginner)
Craft: Canoes, kayaks, rafts
Approximate paddling time: 2 to 4 hours
Flows: 300 to 600 cfs
Season: May through June
Put-in: Cement Creek, at the junction of Highway 135 and Forest Service Road 740
Takeout: Confluence access point off Highway 135, at the confluence of the East and Taylor Rivers

Shuttle: From the junction of Highway 135 and FSR 742 (the takeout), head north on Highway 135 to reach the put-in.

Additional information: Be sure to check out some of the paddling on the nearby Taylor River or on the Upper Gunnison River.

19 Gunnison River

Formed by the confluence of the Taylor and East Rivers just above the Western-flavored town of Gunnison, the Gunnison River begins a sweeping—and dam-filled—course in a northwesterly direction across the Western Slope before joining the Colorado River in Grand Junction (named because of the confluence of these rivers). The Gunnison springs to life for a few miles of beginner-level paddling before falling into the backwaters of Blue Mesa Reservoir, followed by Morrow Point Reservoir, and finally Crystal Reservoir.

Below here the Gunnison tumbles through the dramatic and expert-only Black Canyon of the Gunnison National Monument. As the Gunny eases out of the monument, it courses through the intermediate section known as Gunnison Gorge and finally tapers down through beginner-friendly open farmlands and low-walled sandstone canyons as it eases north toward the Colorado River.

Confluence-Down Section

This uppermost section of the Gunnison is a cruisey nontechnical open-valley paddle for beginning paddlers. Gentle and steady current pushes paddlers past tall cottonwoods, willows, and open ranchlands. This section is mostly away from all roads, and even with numerous homes along the banks, it has a pleasant and lazy rural feel.

Distance: 8.0 miles
Difficulty: Class I-II- (beginner)
Craft: Canoes, kayaks, rafts
Approximate paddling time: 2 to 4 hours
Flows: 300 to 800 cfs
Season: April through September
Put-in: Confluence of the East and Taylor Rivers
Takeout: Twin Bridges
Shuttle: The put-in and takeout are both reached via Highway 135. To reach the takeout, cross the first bridge over the river heading north out of the town of Gunnison. Park in the lot on the west side of the highway.

To reach the put-in, continue heading north on Highway 135 to the river confluence. The put-in is located on the east side of the highway near the town of Almont.

Additional information: Other beginner paddling options are available just upstream of the put-in for this section on both the Lower Taylor and Lower East Rivers.

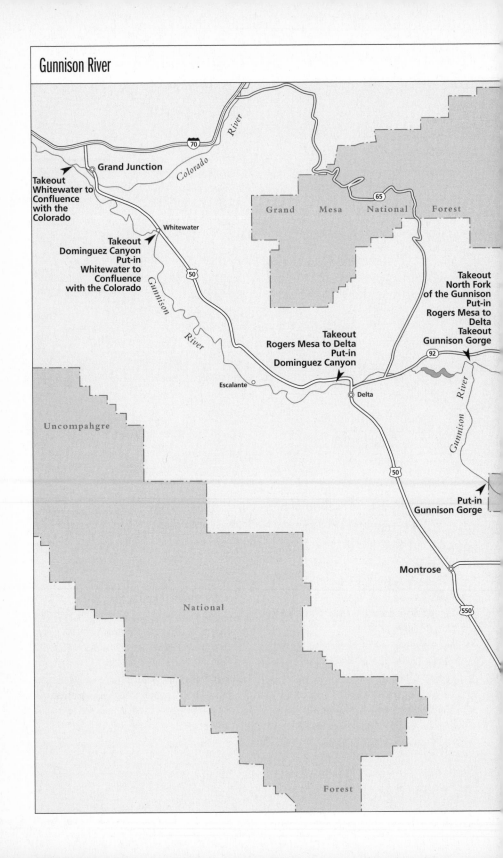

Gunnison River

Takeout
Whitewater to
Confluence
with the
Colorado

Grand Junction

Colorado River

70

Whitewater

Grand Mesa National Forest

65

Takeout
Dominguez Canyon
Put-in
Whitewater to
Confluence
with the Colorado

Gunnison River

50

Escalante

Takeout
Rogers Mesa to Delta
Put-in
Dominguez Canyon

Delta

Takeout
North Fork
of the Gunnison
Put-in
Rogers Mesa to
Delta
Takeout
Gunnison Gorge

92

Gunnison River

Uncompahgre

National

50

Put-in
Gunnison Gorge

Montrose

550

Forest

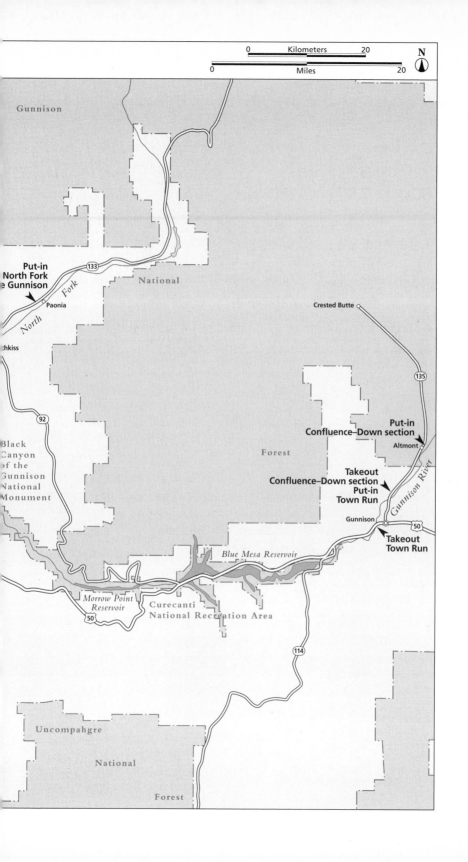

A lone kayaker shreds the surf waves in the Gunnison River Whitewater Park.

Town Run

Considered more a quick and pleasant after-work run, this section is a continuation of the upstream cruisey miles of paddling mentioned above. This section is another great beginner-level run away from the road that passes more ranches and farmlands. Swift current and occasional riffles create a pleasant short paddle for folks looking for a quick get-out-on-the-water experience.

Distance: 4.0 miles
Difficulty: Class I-II- (beginner)
Craft: Canoes, kayaks, rafts
Approximate paddling time: 1 to 2 hours
Flows: 300 to 800 cfs
Season: April through September
Put-in: Twin Bridges, just north of town on Gunnison on Highway 135
Takeout: McCabe's Lane
Shuttle: The put-in is located approximately

5 miles north of town on Highway 135 at the highway bridge that crosses the river. Park in the lot on the northwest side of the river.

To reach the takeout, drive south on Highway 135 into downtown Gunnison and the intersection with U.S. Highway 50. Turn west onto US 50 and continue to the western edge of town. Turn left just after the bridge over the river to the public access area and boat dock at McCabe's Lane.

Additional information: Some paddlers may wish to try surfing and playing in the Gunnison River Whitewater Park located at McCabe's Lane (the takeout for this run). Numerous play features have been constructed and offer some good surfing at early-summer water levels.

Gunnison Gorge

Downstream a ways below the numerous dams and tumultuous Black Canyon lies the pleasant and challenging Gunnison Gorge. The challenge starts right away—a 1.5-mile downhill trail must be navigated before paddlers can dip a blade into the water. Once at the river, steep and arid canyon walls frame good technical intermediate-level whitewater throughout most of the gorge.

The whitewater tends to be abrupt rapids with large rocks to maneuver around and good recovery pools at the bottom of most drops. The crux is found between the Squeeze and the Narrows Rapids as the river cuts through a short dark-colored box canyon. This remote and isolated gorge is home to numerous deer, mountain sheep, beavers, golden and bald eagles, red-tailed hawks, and peregrine falcons. River otters have been sighted here, and countless migratory birds briefly land in the gorge in the shoulder seasons. The waters are home to a healthy population of trout (browns, cutthroats, and rainbows), and many float fishermen make an enjoyable two-day descent of the gorge.

This is a very worthy full-day wilderness paddle that offers great scenery, abundant wildlife, and technical, yet not too stressful whitewater. Enjoy!

Distance: 13.5 miles
Difficulty: Class III–III+ (intermediate)
Craft: Kayaks, rafts
Approximate paddling time: 1 to 2 days
Flows: Dam controlled; 500 to 2,500 cfs
Season: Dam controlled; April through October
Put-in: Chukar Trail
Takeout: Pleasure Park, near the town of Hotchkiss
Shuttle: To reach the put-in, drive north on US 50 approximately 9 miles out of the town of Montrose to Falcon Road. Turn right (east) and continue for 4 miles until Falcon Road becomes Peach Valley Road. Follow Peach Valley Road for approximately 10 miles (can be rough dirt/mud when wet) to a BLM picnic/campground at the Chukar trailhead; this is the put-in.

The takeout is at Pleasure Park, which is located off Highway 92 approximately 6 miles west of the town of Hotchkiss. Turn south at the sign for Forks of the Gunnison and continue for 1 mile to the Pleasure Park takeout area.
Additional information: The folks at Pleasure Park can do shuttles for the Gunny Gorge section. To make arrangements, contact them at (970) 872-2525.

North Fork of the Gunnison

The North Fork of the Gunnison is a swift free-flowing river that offers fairly continuous, shallow current as it passes over and around smaller rocks in its smaller riverbed while cruising past open farmland. Because of its free-flowing nature, it is more challenging with higher early-season runoff and tapers down in swiftness as the water level drops later in the summer. Not an overly big river, the North Fork dries up and is too low for paddling by mid-late summer.

Distance: 15.0 miles
Difficulty: Class II–II- (beginner/intermediate)
Craft: Kayaks, canoes, rafts
Approximate paddling time: 3 to 5 hours
Flows: 500 to 2,000 cfs
Season: April through June
Put-in: Road bridge into Paonia
Takeout: Pleasure Park
Shuttle: The takeout is at Pleasure Park, located off Highway 92 approximately 6 miles west of the town of Hotchkiss. Turn south at the sign for Forks of the Gunnison and continue for 1 mile to the Pleasure Park takeout area.

To reach the put-in, return to Highway 92 and drive approximately 12 miles east to the turnoff for the town of Paonia at Stahl Orchards. In less than 1 mile, the road into town crosses the river; this is the put-in.
Additional information: Check out another beginner-level section of paddling on the Gunnison, just downstream of this takeout. There's an intermediate-level put-in in the town of Somerset (an additional 5 miles).

A pleasant valley with mountain scenery characterizes moderate paddling on the North Fork of the Gunnison River near the town of Paonia.

Rogers Mesa to Delta

This section of the Gunnison is included more for the sake of completeness than for its quality. This section is a mellow, meandering ranchland paddle with open sky and swift current. If you're looking for a full day on the water while in the area, this is a good beginner section.

Distance: 18.0 miles
Difficulty: Class I-II- (beginner)
Craft: Canoes, kayaks, touring/rec boats
Approximate paddling time: 4 to 6 hours
Flows: 500 to 3,000 cfs
Season: April through October; possible year-round
Put-in: Pleasure Park
Takeout: South side of the US 50 bridge in the town of Delta
Shuttle: The put-in is at Pleasure Park, located off Highway 92 approximately 6 miles west of the town of Hotchkiss. Turn south at the sign

for Forks of the Gunnison and continue for 1 mile to the Pleasure Park put-in area.

To reach the takeout, return to Highway 92 and drive west into the town of Delta. At the junction of Highway 92 and US 50, turn right (north) onto US 50. Shortly thereafter, turn left at the south side of the highway bridge over the river; this is the takeout.
Additional information: Check out another beginner level section of paddling on the Lower North Fork of the Gunnison, just upstream of this put-in.

Dominguez Canyon

This section of the Gunnison starts with open ranchland before dropping away from most forms of civilization into an 800-foot-deep, sandstone-walled canyon. Down here the Gunnison offers up pleasant, relatively remote (a railroad parallels the river) beginner-level paddling with swift water, but there's no real rapids above Class II to speak of.

The highlight of this trip is a rewarding hike up Dominguez Canyon (located 10 miles below the Escalante Bridge), where Ancestral Puebloan petroglyphs can be seen up close. In early spring this canyon is a breeding ground for Canada geese, and the cottonwood stands provide rookeries for great blue herons.

Perhaps best suited as a two-day, open-canoe trip, enjoy this last "wilderness" section of the Gunnison.

Distance: Approximately 30.0 miles (shorter run possible)
Difficulty: Class I-II- (beginner)
Craft: Canoes, kayaks, touring/rec boats, rafts
Approximate paddling time: 2 to 3 days
Flows: 500 to 3,000 cfs

Season: March through October; possible year-round
Put-in: US 50 bridge in the town of Delta
Takeout: Highway 141 bridge in the town of Whitewater
Shuttle: See Additional information below

for the most popular put-in for this section. Otherwise use the higher put-in in Delta to add more mileage.

To reach the takeout, head north on US 50 to the little town of Whitewater. Turn west on Highway 141 and follow it to the bridge over the river; this is the takeout.

Additional information: A more frequently used put-in is located at the Escalante Bridge, 10 miles north of Delta on US 50. Turn west at the BLM sign for Escalante Area and continue down a dirt road for 3 miles to the bridge across the river; this is the put-in.

Whitewater to Confluence with the Colorado

Looking for a downstream section to finish off the Gunnison River? Then this is the last hurrah before the Gunnison is swallowed by the larger Colorado. Beginning paddlers start with a bit more canyon for the first few miles before the river opens up into open farmland paddling and ultimately more development as it courses through the growing city of Grand Junction. Swift and steady current offers paddlers a push as they head downstream. Be wary of potential man-made hazards on this section as irrigation canals slurp water out of the river.

Distance: 10.0 miles
Difficulty: Class I-II- (beginner)
Craft: Canoes, kayaks, rafts, touring/rec boats
Time: 2 to 4 hours
Flows: 500 to 3,000 cfs
Season: March through October; possible year-round
Put-in: Highway 141 bridge in the town of Whitewater
Takeout: Near the US 50 bridge, Western Colorado Botanical Gardens
Shuttle: To reach the put-in, head south out of Grand Junction on Highway 50 to the little town of Whitewater. Turn west on Highway 141 and follow it to the bridge that crosses the river; this is the put-in.

To reach the takeout, return to US 50 and head north back into Grand Junction. Just after crossing the Colorado River, follow signs for the botanical gardens. The US 50 bridge at the gardens is the takeout.

Additional information: Beginner level paddling can also be found upstream of the confluence on the Colorado or by continuing downstream (see Colorado River sections for more information on these sections).

20 Lake Fork of the Gunnison River

This small, out-of-the-way tributary to the Gunnison is largely a secret in the realm of Colorado's beginner/intermediate paddlers. Because it is off the "main road" and actually dumps into Blue Mesa Reservoir, it is not easily found by paddlers looking for quality intermediate paddling in the Gunnison area. The free-flowing Lake Fork comes off the north side of the San Juan Mountains. Combining good scenery, easy access, and numerous sections to paddle, the Lake Fork is worth checking out for those looking for a little-known paddling destination.

Box Section

This section of the Lake Fork is located 5 miles north of the quaint, scenic town of Lake City. This piece of river drops down into a 100-foot-deep, steep-walled canyon below the road, committing paddlers to the entire distance of the run. Don't be alarmed—the Box section is little more than sweeping turns of continuous current, with smaller wave trains throughout.

Distance: 11.0 miles
Difficulty: Class II-III- (beginner/intermediate)
Craft: Canoes, kayaks, rafts
Approximate paddling time: 3 to 5 hours
Flows: 400 to 1,000 cfs
Season: Late April through mid-July in most years

Put-in: Ryan's Ranch Bridge
Takeout: Gate Campground
Shuttle: Highway 149 is used for the easy shuttle on the section. Look for the put-in near Mile Marker 79. A sign marks the takeout, located 10 miles north of the put-in.

Gate to Red Bridge Section

This section of the Lake Fork is more of an open-ranchland paddle surrounded by private land on both sides of the river. It is a pleasant beginner-level paddle with a few small waves and defined eddylines, nothing more. Be very wary of landowner issues along this section of river.

Distance: 7.0 miles
Difficulty: Class II (beginner/intermediate)
Craft: Canoes, kayaks, rafts
Approximate paddling time: 2 to 3 hours
Flows: 400 to 1,000 cfs
Season: Late April through mid-July in most years
Put-in: Gate Campground

Takeout: Red Bridge Campground
Shuttle: The put-in is located near Mile Marker 89 on Highway 149.
   To reach the takeout, head north approximately 5 miles to County Road 25. Turn onto this road and continue for 2 miles to the takeout at the campground.

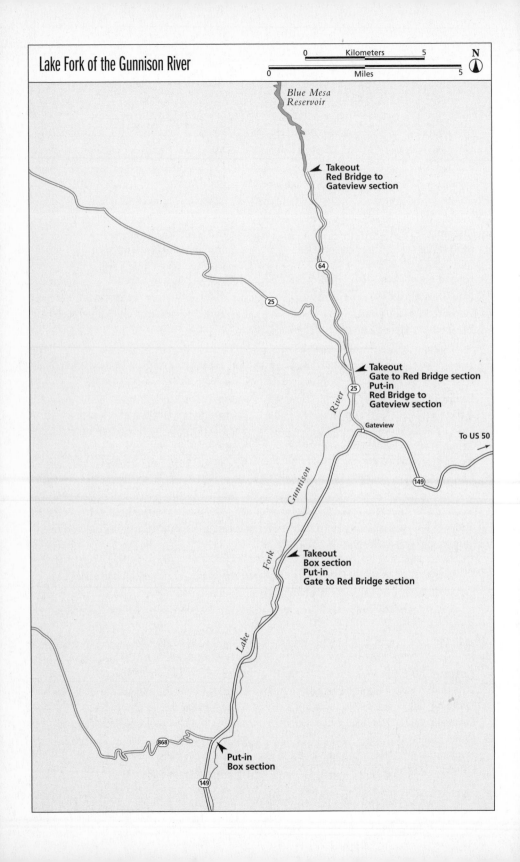

Lake Fork of the Gunnison River

Kilometers
0   5

Miles
0   5

N

Blue Mesa Reservoir

**Takeout
Red Bridge to
Gateview section**

64

25

**Takeout
Gate to Red Bridge section
Put-in
Red Bridge to
Gateview section**

25

River

Gateview

To US 50

149

Gunnison

**Takeout
Box section
Put-in
Gate to Red Bridge section**

Fork

Lake

868

**Put-in
Box section**

149

Red Bridge to Gateview Section

This final section of the Lake Fork provides a challenging and playful intermediate-level run. This section cuts through a nice craggy canyon before all too quickly getting swallowed up by Blue Mesa Reservoir just below the takeout and provides some good whitewater and play features. The crux of the run is Rattlesnake Rapid, located in the middle of the run. This rapid can be easily scouted/portaged from the road along river-right.

Distance: 4.5 miles
Difficulty: Class III (intermediate at lower water levels)
Craft: Kayaks, rafts
Approximate paddling time: 1 to 3 hours
Flows: 400 to 1,000 cfs
Season: Late April through mid-July in most years

Put-in: Red Bridge Campground
Takeout: Gateview Campground
Shuttle: Both the put-in and takeout are reached via CR25. Drive 4 miles north along this dirt road to reach the takeout, which is literally at the end of the road.

21 San Miguel River

The San Miguel tumbles out of the stunning San Juan Mountains directly through the historic mining town of Telluride. More known for its skiing than paddling, downstream of town the river offers up some fine beginner/intermediate paddling options. The largest tributary to the Dolores River, the San Miguel is a cold and free-flowing river due to snowmelt.

Throughout its length before joining the Dolores, the San Miguel makes a transition from alpine/mountain-flavored scenery with a river canyon lined with fir and aspen trees to a desert-flavored, sandstone-walled canyon lined with scrub oak and sagebrush.

Good access and nice paddling options but a short window of runnable flows describes the San Miguel paddling scene.

Sawpit Run

Starting out just below the majestic setting of Telluride, the Upper San Miguel offers a swift-moving section of paddling known as the Sawpit Run. This run features a steady gradient and cold water when it is flowing, so wear those extra layers and put out for a fast ride downstream.

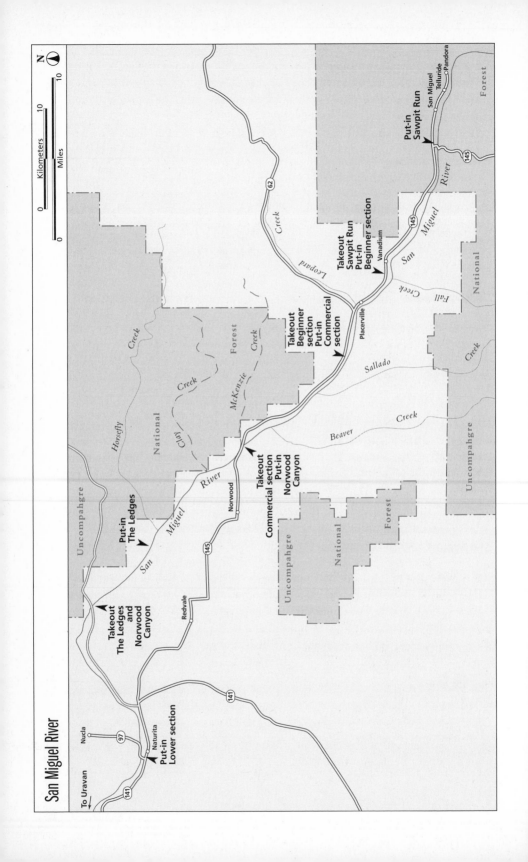

San Miguel River

Smaller waves and rapids dot the earlier portion of this run. The largest rapid—Sawpit (Class III)—lies downstream just above the takeout. Be careful of this run at its highest water levels. It can be a continuous, eddyless flush of a run should the need for rescue occur.

Distance: 7.0 miles
Difficulty: Class II-III (intermediate)
Craft: Rafts, canoes, kayaks
Approximate paddling time: 2 to 3 hours
Flows: 500 to 1,500 cfs
Season: April through June

Put-in: Forest Service Road 625 (Silverpick Road)
Takeout: Fall Creek Road
Shuttle: Follow Highway 145, which parallels the entire section, for both the put-in and takeout.

Beginner Section

Settling down a bit from the upstream run, this section of the San Miguel is a pleasant short paddle for beginners looking to log more river miles. This piece of river is fairly swift, with steady current and no technical rapids to speak of. The length of this run can be easily scouted from Highway 145 while doing shuttle.

Distance: 5.0 miles
Difficulty: Class II (beginner)
Craft: Rafts, canoes, kayaks
Approximate paddling time: 1 to 2 hours
Flows: 500 to 1,500 cfs
Season: April through June

Put-in: Fall Creek Road
Takeout: Specie Creek Recreation Site
Shuttle: Follow Highway 145, which parallels the entire section, for both the put-in and take-out.

Commercial Section

This section of the San Miguel offers visitors to nearby Telluride a commercial raft trip. Not only for paying clients, this is a trip with pleasant scenery, steep hillsides, and sandstone rocks. The river meanders in the bottom of the valley over shallow, continuous rapids and through straightforward wave trains. The length of this run can be easily scouted from Highway 145 while doing the shuttle.

Distance: 8.0 miles
Difficulty: Class II-III (Intermediate)
Craft: Rafts, canoes, kayaks
Approximate paddling time: 2 to 3 hours
Flows: 500 to 1,500 cfs
Season: April through June

Put-in: Specie Creek Recreation Site
Takeout: Norwood Bridge
Shuttle: Follow Highway 145, which parallels the entire section, for both the put-in and takeout.

Norwood Canyon

This section of the San Miguel features the only semi wilderness run away from roads and civilization throughout the river's entire length. At the put-in, the river immediately drops into a wooded canyon flanked by sandstone cliffs. The first 6.0 miles offer easy paddling as you approach Horsefly Creek, entering on river-right. This is a good side hike and an excellent fishing spot.

Below here be wary of a runnable low head dam—run far left. The wilderness seeps away as a small dirt road appears on river-right and continues down to the takeout. This lower portion of the runs features more numerous waves that are great for surfing or charging straight through, depending on your style and skill. All the rapids can be easily negotiated without scouting—a good read and run.

Distance: 16.0 miles
Difficulty: Class II–III (intermediate)
Craft: Rafts, canoes, kayaks
Approximate paddling time: 2 to 3 hours
Flows: 500 to 1,500 cfs
Season: April through June
Put-in: Norwood Bridge
Takeout: Green Truss Bridge

Shuttle: The put-in is located just east of the town of Norwood, down the hill on Highway 145.

To reach the takeout, look for EE30 Road, just after the junction of Highways 145 and 141. Turn right and follow this road uphill, staying to the right until eventually reaching the Green Truss Bridge; this is the takeout.

The Ledges

This section of the San Miguel is actually the last portion of the Norwood Canyon section mentioned previously. It gets its own write-up here largely for the amazing surfing and play waves that develop for paddlers seeking to get their surf on.

Sandstone shelves dropping into the riverbed create uniformly wide surf waves that are very user-friendly. The majority of these can be scouted while bouncing along the dirt road heading to the put-in. This is the play run for Telluride kayakers.

Distance: Approximately 5.0 miles
Difficulty: Class II–III (intermediate)
Craft: Rafts, canoes, kayaks
Approximate paddling time: 2 to 3 hours
Flows: 500 to 1,500 cfs
Season: April through June
Put-in: BB36 Road
Takeout: Green Truss Bridge

Shuttle: From Naturita, head east on Highway 141. Just before the junction of Highways 145 and 141, look for EE30 Road. Turn left and follow this road uphill past the power plant, staying to the right until eventually coming to the Green Truss Bridge; this is the takeout.

Cross the river and head upstream on BB36 Road on river-right to reach the put-in.

A pair of canoeists charges the rewarding whitewater of the Lower San Miguel River.
COURTESY OF CENTENNIAL CANOES

Lower Section

The Lower San Miguel offers pretty straightforward, continuous riffles and current through a rural valley; the riverbanks are lined with cottonwood trees. The infrequently traveled Highway 141 parallels this section, so it is not remote and isolated. But it still offers another section of mellow paddling while you're in the neighborhood.

Distance: 18.0 miles (shorter runs possible)
Difficulty: Class I–II (beginner/intermediate)
Craft: Rafts, canoes, kayaks
Approximate paddling time: 4 to 6 hours
Flows: 500 to 1,500 cfs
Season: April through June
Put-in: County Road 97 bridge in Naturita
Takeout: Confluence with the Dolores River
Shuttle: The easy-to-find put-in is located next to the junction of Highway 141 and CR 97 in Naturita.

To reach the takeout, head downstream (northwest) on Highway 141 to the small town of Uravan. Turn west and cross the river. Continue downstream on a dirt road along river-left to the takeout at the confluence with the Dolores River.

Additional information: For other nearby paddling options, check out the up- and downstream sections of the Dolores River from this section's takeout.

22 Uncompahgre River

The Uncompahgre River starts high in the South San Juan Mountains and flows north into the super-scenic town of Ouray—known as Little Switzerland. As the Uncompahgre flows out of town, it tumbles swiftly and continuously through a very narrow riverbed and then eases a bit above the town of Ridgway as it passes continuous ranchland with barbed wire lacing the river. At the pleasant small town of Ridgway, the Uncompahgre is finally recommended for paddling.

Lower Run

This section of the Uncompahgre starts right in the middle of Ridgway with a few nice man-made ledges to paddle through or use for warm-up surfing. Below here the river meanders a few miles through a relatively open valley lined with cottonwood trees before dropping into a shallow, steep-sided section with more technical rapids. This fun, quick run provides some on-the-fly play opportunities before dropping into the backwaters of Ridgway Reservoir.

Distance: 5.0 miles
Difficulty: Class II (intermediate)
Craft: Kayaks, rafts, canoes
Approximate paddling time: 1 to 2 hours
Flows: 250 to 900 cfs
Season: Late April through late June
Put-in: Highway 62 bridge in the town of Ridgway
Takeout: Dallas Creek access in Ridgway State Park
Shuttle: The put-in is located just below the Highway 62 bridge in Ridgway.

To reach the takeout, head north out of Ridgway on U.S. Highway 550. After 5 miles look for a sign for Ridgway State Park. Turn left (west) into the park and pay the entrance fee. Turn left at the first junction and follow signs to the takeout at the Dallas Creek access.

Additional information: Paddlers may wish to spend time at the put-in surfing and playing in the numerous man-made river features. A river trail parallels the entire section for bike/running shuttle options.

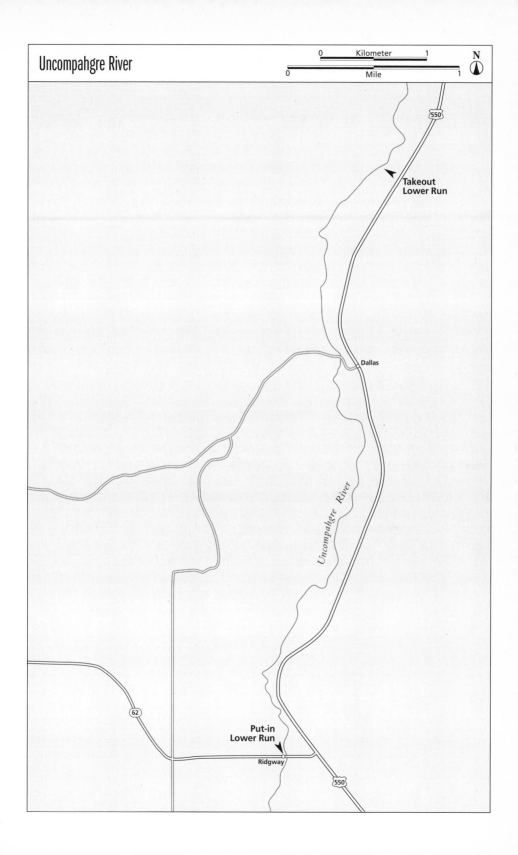

Uncompahgre River

23 Dolores River

Talk about a river that goes through a transition. The Dolores River indeed covers some distance and varied terrain as it makes it way out of the aspen forests off the west side of the San Juan Mountains before flowing northwest into Utah and joining the Colorado River just above the sandstone-covered town of Moab.

Free flowing in its upper reaches, the Upper Dolores follows a short but steady course until it flows into the backwaters of McPhee Reservoir. Unfortunately this reservoir has been disastrous in terms of offering adequate and consistent boatable flows downstream of the dam. When, in big snowmelt/runoff years, the dam releases sufficient water to provide the recommended level for paddling, the Lower Dolores offers numerous remote, multiday sections for beginning/intermediate desert-loving paddlers looking to get away from it all for a while.

Upper River to Stoner Section

Here the Upper Dolores River flows through a beautiful high-mountain, aspen-filled valley. It is free flowing at this point and so flows strong, fast, and cold when it is flowing strong in early summer. The majority of this section offers up straightforward continuous waves and steady current, but little technical difficulty. Be careful in higher water—steady, continuous current can make swimming and rescuing boats a long and unpleasant experience.

In the heart of the run, a section of great surf waves offers the most technical features. You can charge through them if surfing is not your thing. Sloping sandstone bedrock shelves form an even river bottom that creates shallow surf waves. After this section, the Dolores settles back down and finishes off in the beautiful little hamlet of Stoner.

Distance: 14.0 miles
Difficulty: Class II–III (intermediate)
Craft: Kayaks
Time: 3 to 5 hours
Flows: Free flowing; 500 to 2,000 cfs
Season: Late April through late June in most years
Put-in: Roaring Forks Creek
Takeout: Stoner Bridge
Shuttle: Use Highway 145 for both the put-in (near Mile Marker 34) and the takeout (near Mile Marker 21).

Additional information: The best intermediate surf waves/play spots on this section are found between Mile Markers 29 and 26 for a short, wham-bam, 3.0-mile-long, Class III play run known as the Stampede. Beginning paddlers can put in at Stoner and continue downstream to the town of Dolores for an additional 15.0 miles of Class II water. Numerous roadside pullouts provide easy access.

◄ *A pair of kayakers shreds the man-made surf waves on the Uncompahgre River in Ridgeway.*

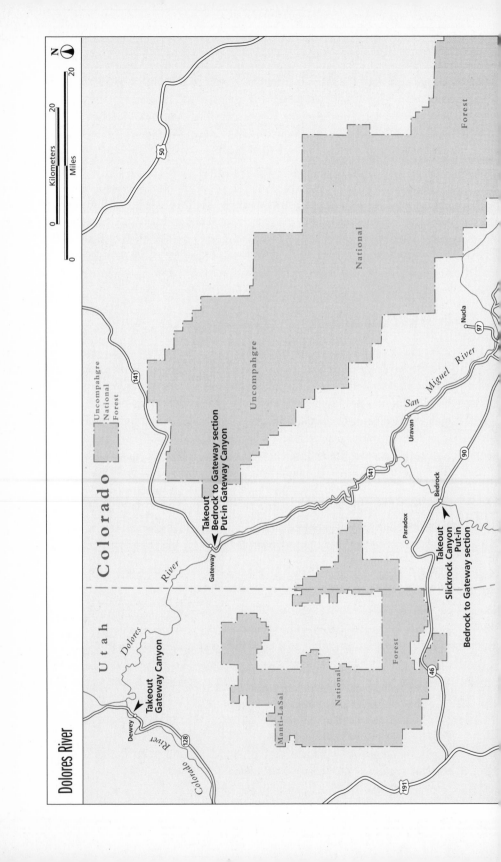

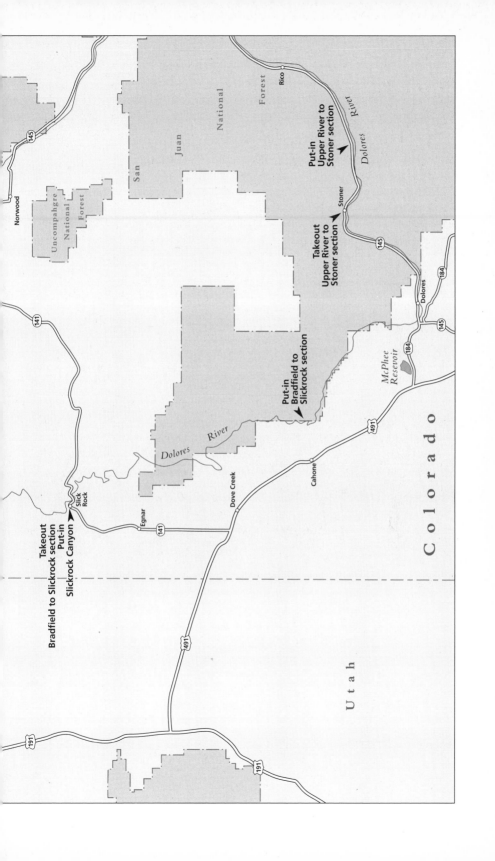

A group of kayakers enjoys the run out of Snaggletooth Rapid in Dolores Canyon.

Bradfield to Slickrock Section

Because of the unfortunate operations of McPhee Dam just upstream of the put-in, this section of the Dolores River is perhaps one of the best but least paddled intermediate multiday river trips in the West. Catching this section with ample flow is the challenge, but once the water is flowing, paddlers will thoroughly enjoy a Douglas fir-, ponderosa pine-, and juniper-lined canyon in the upper parts of this run. Up here the canyon reaches almost 2,500 feet in depth. It is easy to find a pleasant campsite beneath the towering sandstone walls and pleasant trees.

The river cruises along with steady current and fairly straightforward rapids that fall in the Class II–II+ range, mostly found on corners and at the mouth of side canyons. The canyon was once home to Ancestral Puebloans, and cliffside remnants can be seen just below Glade Canyon on river-right. After the river makes a sweeping turn to the north around Mountain Sheep Point, the whitewater picks up. Lunchbox and Molar Rapids provide a warm-up before the big one—Snaggletooth Rapid (Class IV). This chunky rapid can easily be scouted and portaged on a dirt track on river-left.

Below this drop the Dolores keeps charging northward through Wall and Mile Long Rapids (both Class III). After these rapids the canyon makes a noticeable transition to a more open feel. Scrub oak, sagebrush, and cacti are the primary vegetation. The river then settles down as it drifts placidly for the last 8.0 miles or so to the takeout.

Distance: 47.0 miles

Difficulty: Class III–IV (intermediate)

Craft: Rafts, canoes, kayaks

Approximate paddling time: 3 to 4 days

Flows: Dam-controlled; 500 to 2,000 cfs

Season: Dam-controlled; April through May

Put-in: Bradfield launch site

Takeout: Slick Rock

Shuttle: To reach the put-in, travel west on U.S. Highway 491 out of Cortez. In the small town of Cahone, turn right (east), following signs to Bradfield launch site onto County Road R. Follow CR R approximately 3 miles and then turn right onto County Road 16. Go approximately 1.5 miles, turn left onto County Road S, and continue into the access area to put in.

To reach the takeout, return to Highway 491 heading west through the town of Dove Creek. Look for Highway 141, which heads north just after town. Follow Highway 141 across the plateau through little Egnar and then drop down into the river canyon and use the bridge across the river near the town of Slick Rock as the takeout. Park in the lot on the north side of the river, upstream of the bridge.

Additional information: No river permit is needed on this river. To find out about flows, contact the BLM office in Durango at (970) 247-4874.

Slickrock Canyon

The Slickrock Canyon section of the Dolores River offers up a mellower multiday desert-flavored trip through an intimate canyon. This is a great open-canoe trip.

If you put in at Slick Rock, the river starts slowly and wanders through ranchland. (A lower put-in is available at the entrance to the canyon; see below for details.) Once entering the canyon, the river sweeps and meanders around tight corners flanked by sheer-walled sandstone cliffs. This means that campsites are sparse and not the largest size. Piñon, juniper, and prickly pear are the main vegetation in the canyon.

Swift current carries paddlers easily downstream at good water levels, and smaller rapids (nothing more than Class II) are found at the mouth of side canyons that enter the river. There's a good campsite and a side hike opportunity at Spring Canyon, which enters on river-right in the middle of the canyon. Three miles downstream is Coyote Wash, which enters on river-left and affords the best campsite in the canyon, as well as a short side hike that leads to Ancestral Puebloan rock art. If the campsite is already taken, at least stop and go for a side hike to check out the petroglyphs. Below here is a nice day's paddle to the takeout at the classically Western Bedrock Store.

Distance: 50.0 miles
Difficulty: Class II (beginner/intermediate)
Craft: Rafts, canoes, kayaks
Approximate paddling time: 2 to 3 days
Flows: Dam-controlled; 500 to 2,000 cfs
Season: Dam-controlled; April to May
Put-in: Highway 141 bridge, Slick Rock
Takeout: Highway 90 bridge, Bedrock
Shuttle: The put-in is located at the river access area at the Highway 141 bridge in the town of Slick Rock. Highway 141 is off Highway 491 just west of the town of Dove Creek.

To reach the takeout, continue heading north on Highway 141 through the town of Naturita.

Just west of town look for signs for Highway 90; turn left (west) and follow Highway 90 through Paradox Valley to the river bridge and takeout in Bedrock. The actual takeout is located upstream on river-left.

Additional information: A lower put-in near the entrance to Slick Rock Canyon is often used at Gypsum launch site. This avoids 15 miles of flatwater that passes relatively uninteresting ranchland. No permits are required for this run. For additional information regarding flows, contact the BLM office in Durango at (970) 247-4874.

Bedrock to Gateway Section

This section of the Dolores is no true wilderness like the upstream runs, as lesser used roads parallel the length of this section. This stretch is, however, equally pleasant in terms of its sandstone-walled scenery and beginner/intermediate-friendly paddling.

Starting out in the open Paradox Valley, the Dolores below the put-in eases downstream before cutting into a brief 5.0-mile-long canyon upstream of the San Miguel River confluence that offers rapids up to an easy Class III. Below the confluence the Dolores doubles in size with increased flow and enters into the deep, steep, red-walled

Mesa Canyon. The canyon is relatively tranquil all the way down to Gateway, with no rapids above Class II. Historical sites abound within this peaceful canyon—remnants of a hanging water flume built in 1890 are easily seen along the canyon wall.

Even though Highway 141 parallels the river, it is on the canyon rim way above the river and offers little intrusion.

Distance: 44.0 miles total (shorter runs possible)

Difficulty: Class II–III (intermediate)

Craft: Rafts, canoes, kayaks

Approximate paddling time: 2 to 4 days (shorter runs possible)

Flows: Dam-controlled on the Dolores. The San Miguel is free flowing; 700 to 3,000 cfs.

Season: April through June in most years (check flows on the Dolores)

Put-in: Bedrock launch site

Takeout: Gateway access site

Shuttle: To reach the put-in, travel to the town of Bedrock on Highway 90. The actual access point for launching is just upstream of the bridge on river-left.

To reach the takeout, briefly head east on Highway 90. In less than 1 mile from Bedrock, turn left (north) onto River Road (dirt), which parallels the river to the confluence with the San Miguel River. Just upstream of the confluence on River Road, turn left (west) onto Highway 141 and continue downstream above the river to the town of Gateway. Look for BLM access signs for the takeout just upstream of the bridge.

Additional information: Roads parallel much of the length of this section, so shorter runs are possible with various access points along the way. Check out upstream runs on the San Miguel River for other paddling options.

Gateway Canyon

This is the last canyon section of the Dolores River before it dumps into the Colorado River just across the Utah border. The river cruises downstream of the put-in in a wide valley with a dirt road following the first 8.0 miles down to the biggest rapid of this section—Stateline Rapid (Class III at lower water levels, up to Class III+–IV at higher water levels).

The canyon walls begin to squeeze in here, and the river tumbles through a long island rapid that requires a scout on river-right. Below here the river officially enters into Gateway Canyon and the whitewater picks up in frequency. Be aware of Beaver Falls—another technical, boulder-filled Class III rapid—at the mouth of Beaver Creek outwash, which enters from river-left. The river then bends back to the north, and the canyon is at its narrowest and most dramatic point down here in the heart of Gateway Canyon far away from it all.

Multiple side canyons offer pleasant off-river hiking options through this section of the canyon. Eventually the Dolores comes out of the intimate canyon and slowly flows across broad open lands till it joins the mighty Colorado. Only 1 mile downstream of this confluence is the historic Dewey suspension bridge. The takeout is upstream of the bridge on river-right.

Distance: 32.0 miles
Difficulty: Class II–III (III+) (intermediate)
Craft: Rafts, canoes, kayaks
Approximate paddling time: 2 to 3 days
Flows: 700 to 3,000 cfs
Season: April through late June in most years
Put-in: Gateway launch site
Takeout: Dewey Bridge on Highway 128 in Utah
Shuttle: This is a long but reliable shuttle if using Highway 141 east from the put-in through Grand Junction, then Interstate 70 west, and then Highway 128 south to Dewey Bridge takeout.

A more rugged (and possibly closed due to spring snow) option is to take County Road 44 from the put-in heading west to the junction with Forest Service Road 207. Turn right (west) onto the Castleton Valley Road, then right (north) at the Highway 128 (Utah) junction to Dewey Bridge.

Additional information: For additional information, contact the BLM office in Moab at (435) 259-7012.

24 San Juan River

The San Juan River falls off the south side of Wolf Creek Pass in the southwest corner of the state just above the scenic town of Pagosa Springs. Wolf Creek Pass is often the location for the highest recorded snowfall in the state each winter. What this means is that the free-flowing Upper San Juan bursts to life with cold, fast, high water every snowmelt season. Paddlers can find the highest sections of paddling on the West Fork, as well as a brief section on the East Fork.

The Upper San Juan officially starts at the East Fork and West Fork confluence 10 miles above the town of Pagosa Springs. Below this confluence the river eases through a broad valley as it approaches town. Below town the San Juan drops into a more remote section known as Mesa Canyon. This stretch offers a nice day of paddling in a more remote setting with intermediate whitewater.

Below this section the San Juan eases slowly for miles before it drops into the backwaters of Navajo Reservoir, where it is dammed. These sections of the Upper San Juan, while still in Colorado, offer fine beginner/intermediate paddling in more of a forested landscape. The Lower San Juan offers the same style of paddling, but in a sandstone-desert environment.

West Fork Section

This section of the Lower West Fork of the San Juan offers a short, swift sampling of busy intermediate paddling set in a beautiful valley. This section has no real distinguished rapids to speak of, but it still has wave trains and swift current at higher water levels. With snow-covered peaks as a backdrop, the West Fork can be a scenic higher put-in point for those looking to paddle all the way back down into town.

Be aware of private property and large ranches along side the river on this section.

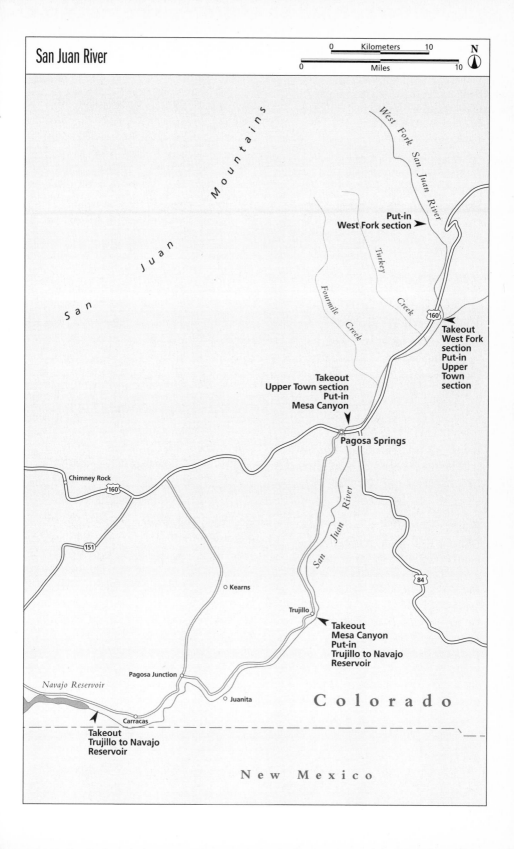

San Juan River

Kilometers 10
0
0
Miles 10
N

Put-in
West Fork section

West Fork San Juan River

Turkey Creek

Fourmile Creek

160

Takeout
West Fork
section
Put-in
Upper
Town
section

Takeout
Upper Town section
Put-in
Mesa Canyon

Pagosa Springs

San Juan River

Chimney Rock

160

151

Kearns

84

Trujillo

Takeout
Mesa Canyon
Put-in
Trujillo to Navajo
Reservoir

Pagosa Junction

Juanita

C o l o r a d o

Navajo Reservoir

Carracas

Takeout
Trujillo to Navajo
Reservoir

N e w   M e x i c o

Distance: 5.0 miles
Difficulty: Class II (advanced beginner/intermediate)
Craft: Whitewater kayaks, canoes, rafts
Approximate paddling time: 1 to 3 hours
Flows: 200 to 800 cfs
Season: April through July
Put-in: West Fork Campground
Takeout: U.S. Highway 160 bridge
Shuttle: Use US 160 heading north out of Pagosa Springs as the main shuttle route for this section. Ten miles north of town, US 160 crosses over the river. Turn right (east) immediately after the bridge onto a dirt road. Continue down this dirt road a short distance to the takeout just below the confluence with the East Fork.

To reach the put-in, return to US 160 and turn right (north). Look for Forest Service Road 648 (West Fork Road) just before Treasure Falls. Turn left (west) onto this road and follow it to the bridge over the river and the West Fork trailhead and Campground; this is the put-in.

Upper Town Section

This section of the San Juan features swift, constant current and straightforward wave train rapids largely found on the bends in the river course. The higher the water level, the faster—and eddyless—the ride down into town. This is especial noticeable due to the doubling of the river's flow below the put-in confluence. The majority of the harder whitewater (Class III) is found in the beginning of the run, and it tapers down in difficulty as the river approaches town.

This is mostly a scenic paddle through a narrow river channel that is lined with large ranches and horse pastures. US 160 closely parallels the majority of this section, so it has more of a rural feel than a true remote feeling. Private property lines both sides of the river for the duration of this section, so please be conscious of this if you need to step ashore for any reason.

Distance: 10.0 miles
Difficulty: Class II–III (intermediate)
Craft: Whitewater kayaks, canoes, rafts
Approximate paddling time: 2 to 4 hours
Flows: 300 to 1,500 cfs
Season: April through July
Put-in: Confluence of East Fork and West Fork
Takeout: Visitor center
Shuttle: Use US 160 heading north out of Pagosa Springs as the main shuttle route for this section. Ten miles north of town, US 160 crosses the river. Turn right (east) immediately after the bridge onto a dirt road. Continue down this dirt road a short distance to the put-in just below the confluence with the East Fork.

To reach the takeout, return to town. Turn left at the first traffic light and follow signs for the visitor center.

Additional information: More playful paddlers may wish to check out the man-made play wave just below the takeout, directly across from the hot springs. A good eddy-serviced surf wave is found here at most levels.

Happy rafters enjoy the fun Upper Town section of the San Juan River.
COURTESY OF PAGOSA OUTSIDE

Mesa Canyon

Paddling through town has a bit of an urban feel to it initially, but shortly below town the river drops away from it all into scenic Mesa Canyon. The riverbanks are lined with ponderosa pines, piñons, and junipers. Ample raptors can be seen, such as red-tailed hawks and golden eagles.

The riverbanks are shared between Forest Service land in the top portion of the run and Southern Ute Indian Tribe land on the lower part. The crux of the run is Rock Garden Rapid (Class III-) near the mouth of Squaw Canyon about halfway through the run.

Eventually the canyon opens up near Mile 10, and paddlers ease their way down to the takeout.

Distance: 16.0 miles
Difficulty: Class II–III (advanced beginner/ intermediate)
Craft: Whitewater kayaks, canoes, rafts
Approximate paddling time: 3 to 6 hours
Flows: 500 to 2,000 cfs

Season: April through July
Put-in: Visitor center
Takeout: Bridge in Trujillo
Shuttle: From the visitor center located in downtown Pagosa Springs, head west on US 160 through town. Still in downtown, turn left

(south) at a traffic light onto County Road 500. Follow CR 500 out of town as it becomes dirt and eventually parallels the river near the end of this run. Approaching the hamlet of Trujillo, CR 500 crosses the river; this is the takeout.

Trujillo to Navajo Reservoir

Once the Upper San Juan comes out of Mesa Canyon just upstream of the town of Trujillo, the remaining course flows through a broad valley lined with lush stands of cottonwoods and large ranches before entering into the stagnant waters of Navajo Reservoir. This is mostly a flatwater section, with occasional riffles and smaller waves found at higher water levels.

Because of the relatively isolated valley, dirt-road shuttle, and few people around, this lower section of the Upper San Juan is a quiet, little-paddled run that is very good for canoes.

Distance: 28.0 miles (shorter runs possible)
Difficulty: Class II (beginner/intermediate)
Craft: Kayaks, canoes, rafts
Approximate paddling time: Varies depending on length of run
Flows: 500 to 2,000 cfs
Season: April through August
Put-in: Bridge in Trujillo
Takeout: Navajo Reservoir
Shuttle: In downtown Pagosa Springs, look for CR 500 and head south toward Trujillo. Starting in Trujillo, CR 500 parallels the river.

The river channel can be easily scouted, and numerous pullouts can be used for intermediate access points depending on your desired distance and time.

Additional information: From Trujillo to Pagosa Junction, the river is mostly Class I+, with a few easy Class II rapids. Below Pagosa Junction, the river is easier, with mostly Class I current. A little-used dirt road parallels the river and offers numerous access points for intermediate put-ins or takeouts.

25 Piedra River

Piedra River literally means "river of rocks," as early Spanish explorers aptly named it. Flowing southward out of the Weminuche Wilderness Area (the largest wilderness area in Colorado) and off the Continental Divide, the Piedra is a free-flowing torrent that's fast and cold with early-season snowmelt.

The Piedra is a technical little gem of a river that offers remote intermediate paddling in its upper reaches, a challenging lower gorge for advanced paddlers, and a mellow rural section before dumping into the backwaters of Navajo Reservoir, which dams the San Juan River.

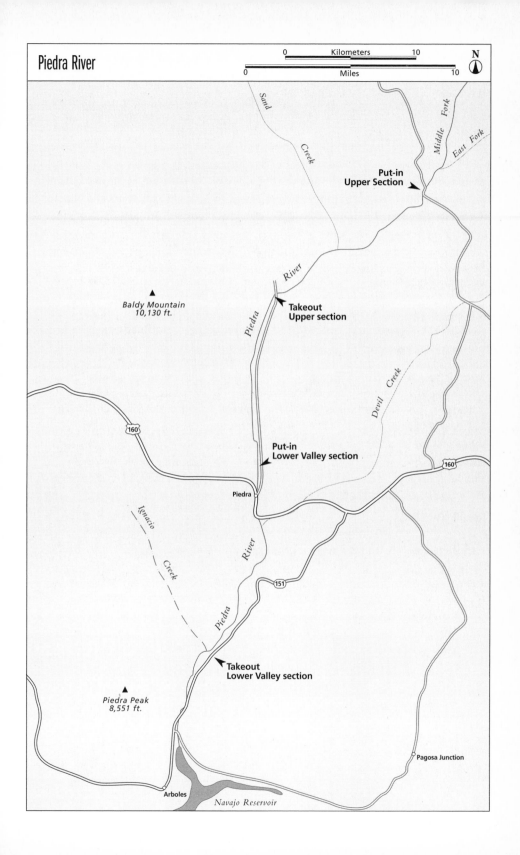

Upper Section

With snow-covered peaks as a put-in backdrop, this upper section of the Piedra is a beautiful remote run with technical intermediate whitewater. Shortly below the put-in, the Piedra drops into a tight canyon where wilderness abounds. Paddlers have seen deer, elk, bear, and wild turkey through this section.

Numerous side creeks enter into the river and boost its flow as it heads downstream. The bigger rapids of this section (Lone Pine and Limestone, both Class III) are found in a lower box canyon. This wild and scenic section of river is not to be missed if it's flowing when you're in the area.

Distance: 10.5 miles
Difficulty: Class II–III (intermediate)
Craft: Whitewater kayaks, canoes, rafts
Approximate paddling time: 2 to 4 hours
Flows: 500 to 2,000 cfs
Season: April through late June
Put-in: Piedra Road bridge
Takeout: First Fork Bridge/Campground
Shuttle: To reach the put-in, head 2 miles west of downtown Pagosa Springs on U.S. Highway 160. Turn right (north) onto Piedra River Road (Forest Service Road 631) and follow it for 16 miles until it crosses the river; this bridge is the put-in.

To reach the takeout, return to US 160 and turn right (west). Continue for 19 miles to First Fork Road, just before the US 160 bridge over the river. Turn right (north) onto First Fork Road and continue upstream for 10 miles to the takeout at the First Fork Bridge/Campground.
Additional information: Just downstream of the takeout for this section, the Piedra drops into the First Box Gorge—a committing and technical Class IV section for advanced/expert paddlers.

Lower Valley Section

This is the tame and mellow section of the upstream gorge runs of the Piedra. Nothing ever reaches above Class II as swift current and shallow water pull paddlers downstream with little effort. This lower run is a more open valley that floats past cottonwood, ranches, and horse property.

Be wary of possible man-made hazards such as barbed wire strung across the river in places, as both sides of the river are private property. Paddlers can continue all the way down into the beginning of Navajo Reservoir as a lowest point takeout. Higher access points can easily be used just off the road that parallels the lower portion of this run.

Tony Miely navigates the Crux Rapid on the ▶
Upper Piedra River.

Distance: 16.0 miles (shorter runs possible)

Difficulty: Class II (advanced beginner/intermediate)

Craft: Whitewater kayaks, canoes, rafts

Approximate paddling time: 2 to 4 hours

Flows: 500 to 2,000 cfs

Season: April to late June

Put-in: Dirt pullout 1 mile upstream of US 160 on river-left

Takeout: Dirt pullout off County Road 151

Shuttle: To reach the put-in, head east on US 160 from the highway bridge over the river. Turn left (north) onto the first dirt road just after the bridge and head upstream 1 mile to the put-in at a dirt pullout on the left side of the road.

To reach the takeout, return to US 160 and turn left (east). Turn right (south) onto CR 151 and follow this road until it parallels the lower portion of the run. Numerous dirt pullouts can be used for takeout points, or paddlers may continue down to the Piedra River access point at the head of Navajo Reservoir.

26 Animas River

The free-flowing Animas River tumbles downhill in a cold, swift torrent off the south side of the San Juan Mountains in the remote southwest corner of Colorado. The Animas begins its navigability in the town of Silverton as it drops through the expert-only Upper Animas Gorge—a cold, continuous 25 miles of thrilling whitewater set beneath snow-covered peaks.

The Animas is literally choked between sheer walls as it exits out of the mountains just above Durango. It settles down through peaceful meanderings in a wide valley offering miles of great flatwater river touring. As the Animas flows into town, it picks up some speed and offers a good short commercial rafting run through town, as well as a great after-work, rinse-off section for playboaters.

Below Durango the Animas settles into a friendly but busy pace as it flows out of the state and joins the San Juan River just across the New Mexico border.

Upper Valley Section

This section is the first piece of river that can be accessed by beginning paddlers as the Animas slows from its dramatic downhill charge just upstream. This section begins with some current just below the put-in and gradually slows as it cruises through the wide-open Upper Animas Valley. Paddlers pass some rather large and glorious riverside homesteads as well as open ranchlands lined with occasional cottonwood trees. This is a great family float and a shorter beginner run than the section just downstream.

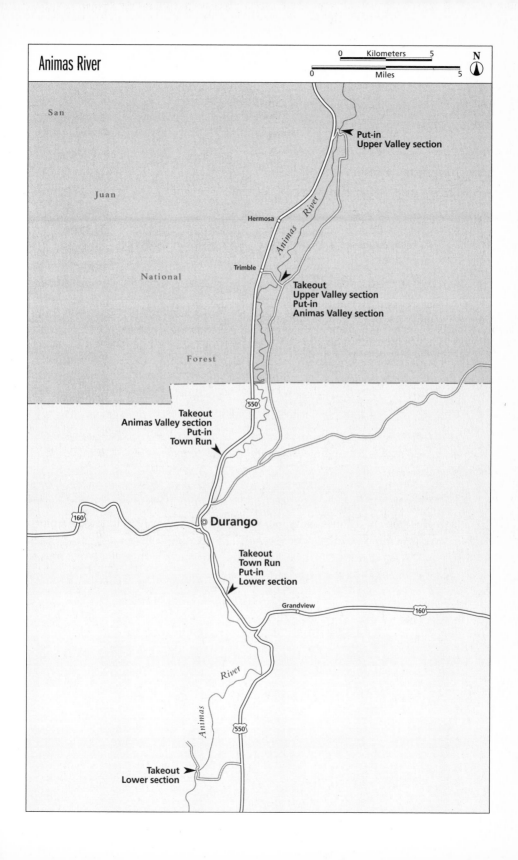

Distance: 8.0 miles
Difficulty: Class I (beginner)
Craft: Canoes, kayaks, touring/rec boats
Approximate paddling time: 2 to 4 hours
Flows: 500 to 3,000 cfs
Season: Year-round
Put-in: Baker's Bridge on County Road 250
Takeout: Trimble Lane
Shuttle: Using U.S. Highway 550 as the main road for the shuttle, head north out of Her-mosa (8 miles north of Durango) and look for signs for CR 250. Turn right (east) onto CR 250 and follow it down to the put-in at the bridge over the river.

To reach the takeout, return to US 550 and head south through Hermosa. Look for Trimble Lane just to the south. Turn left (east) and follow this road to the takeout at the bridge over the river.

A family enjoys a pleasant evening float on the Lower Animas Valley section of the Animas River just above Durango.
COURTESY OF PERFORMANCE VIDEO

Animas Valley Section

If you're looking for a longer section of river for a family float or a great river touring section, then here you go. Meandering miles of flatwater offer paddlers a scenic cruise in the wide-open Animas Valley as the river floats beneath sandstone cliffs in the distance while passing by open ranchland and horse properties.

Higher water will help push paddlers downstream; lower water tends to be a bit more of a slog and a long flatwater paddle. Wave to tourists—the historic and famous Durango-Silverton Narrow Gauge Railroad parallels part of this section of river.

Distance: 13.0 miles
Difficulty: Class I (beginner)
Craft: Canoes, kayaks, touring/rec boats
Approximate paddling time: 4 to 6 hours
Flows: 500 to 3,000 cfs
Season: Year-round; high water May through June
Put-in: Trimble Lane
Takeout: 32nd Street boat ramp

Shuttle: Use US 550 as the main road for the shuttle, heading north out of Durango. Turn right (east) onto Trimble Lane and follow it to the put in at the bridge over the river.

To reach the takeout, return to US 550 and head south back into town. Turn left (east) onto 32nd Street and cross the river. Make an immediate left (north) and go 1 block to the boat ramp; this is the takeout.

Town Run

The Animas literally flows through the middle of town and offers a watery route from the north end to the south end. The put-in offers a good flatwater warm-up for beginning paddlers as the river eases the first few miles downstream. Just below a fish hatchery on river-right, the whitewater picks up a bit and continues swiftly downstream, with a rapid just under the railroad bridge as well as the Main Street bridge.

The real crux of the section is found below the U.S. Highway 160 bridge as paddlers approach Little Smelter Rapid. Big Smelter Rapid (Class III) is found downstream in Santa Rita Park. This is the site of many a swim for budding paddlers, as well as a test of skills for numerous playboaters and slalom racers.

Just below Smelter Rapid, the Animas tumbles around the corner, heading through Korner Pocket Rapid. Farther downstream the river flows over Santa Rita Hole just underneath the US 160 and River Trail bridges. This rapid marks the last of the big ones. The river settles down a bit through Sawmill and High Bridge Rapids farther downstream.

Various put-ins and takeouts can be used to shorten this section or lessen the difficulty based on paddlers' skill levels.

Distance: 5.0 miles
Difficulty: Class II–III (beginner/intermediate)
Craft: Whitewater kayaks/canoes, rafts
Approximate paddling time: 2 to 4 hours
Flows: 300 to 3,000 cfs
Season: Best flows April through July; possible year-round at low flows
Put-in: 32nd Street boat ramp
Takeout: Dalla River Park
Shuttle: Use US 550/Main Street as the main route for the shuttle to the put-in. Head north from downtown to 32nd Street. Turn right (east) onto 32nd Street and cross the river. Make an immediate left (north) and go 1 block to the put in at the boat ramp.

To reach the takeout, head south on Main Street and veer to the right, following signs for US 550 just past a Burger King. Stay on US 550/160 east as the road heads past a Wal-Mart on the right. Shortly thereafter turn right (south) onto River Road next to a Home Depot. Head down to the river, cross over it, and then turn right into the newly constructed Dalla River Park.

Additional information: Beginning paddlers can shorten this section by taking out at the fish hatchery. More playful paddlers can shorten this section by using Santa Rita Park as a put-in and taking out behind Four Corners Riversports to access the best play waves.

Lower Section

This lower section of the Animas offers a scenic paddle south of town with busy water but no real rapids to speak of. With the rapids upstream, paddlers can enjoy this section of swift water, occasional rocks, and wide-open views as the Animas settles down in a pleasant valley before it joins the San Juan River farther downstream.

About halfway through this run, the Animas enters the Southern Ute Indian Reservation. Permits are not required for floating through their land but are required for parking or using their access point at the takeout. For permit information call the Southern Ute Tribe at (970) 563-4525.

Distance: 11.5 miles
Difficulty: Class I–II (beginner/intermediate)
Craft: Whitewater kayaks, canoes, rafts
Approximate paddling time: 3 to 5 hours
Flows: 500 to 3,000 cfs
Season: Best flows April through July; possible year-round at low flows
Put-in: Dalla River Park
Takeout: Weaselskin Bridge

Shuttle: To reach the put-in, head just east of the Home Depot on US 550/160 and turn south onto River Road. Cross the river and turn right at the T into the parking lot for the boat ramp.

To reach the takeout, head downstream at the T, which is La Posta Road. Continue downstream for approximately 10 miles to the takeout at Weaselskin Bridge.

Toby Scarpella gives commands to his parents, Alison and Brian, while kicking back on Vallecito Reservoir.

Flatwater Tours— Lakes and Reservoirs

(North–South)

In addition to its rivers and creeks, Colorado also possesses numerous reservoirs and lakes that offer abundant opportunities for flatwater tours. Many of these paddles feature majestic mountain backdrops, as well as relative seclusion away from most traffic.

Access is great throughout most of the state's reservoirs, as many of them feature state parks and designated launch areas. This section highlights a few of the more popular lakes and reservoirs for flatwater touring plus some other noteworthy locations. If looking for some easy paddling for the whole family, Colorado's lakes and reservoirs offer some great paddling options.

27 Horsetooth Reservoir

Lying just on the west side of Fort Collins, Horsetooth Reservoir is a fine location for a leisurely paddling tour. Set beneath the aptly named Horsetooth Rock, this 1,900+-acre reservoir offers a pleasant tour within close proximity to downtown. A busy, motor-laden boat ramp is located on the south side of the reservoir, but the more isolated north end is more appealing to recreational paddlers. Using the easy access and amenities within Lory State Park on the northwest side of the reservoir, paddlers will find a good boat launch for an afternoon tour.

Head south along the western side of the lake to get away from all the roads. Explore the numerous small coves (Soldier, North Eltuck, South Eltuck, and Orchard) along this steep, hilly side of the reservoir and enter Horsetooth Mountain Park just to the south. Numerous nearby trails are also available for stretching out your legs after a paddle.

Distance: 1.0 to 5.0 miles (as long as desired)
Launch site: Satanka Bay boat ramp
Craft: Rec boats, canoes, kayaks
Approximate paddling time: 1 to 3 hours
Season: April through October; year-round possible
Access: From downtown Fort Collins, head south on U.S. Highway 287 to Drake Road. Turn right (west) onto Drake Road and continue until a T-intersection with South Overland Trail. Turn right (north) onto South Overland Trail, and then very shortly turn left (west) onto County Road 38E. Take this uphill to the edge

of the reservoir and another T-intersection. Turn right onto County Road 23, which parallels the eastern edge of the reservoir. Follow CR 23 all the way around the northern edge of the reservoir to Lory State Park. Pay the entrance and follow signs for the Satanka Bay boat ramp; this is the launch site.
Additional information: For more information on Lory State Park, visit http://parks.state .co.us/Parks/lory. For information on Horsetooth Reservoir, call (970) 679-4554.
Honorable mentions: Boyd Lake State Park, south of Fort Collins; the western edge of Carter Lake, southwest of Loveland.

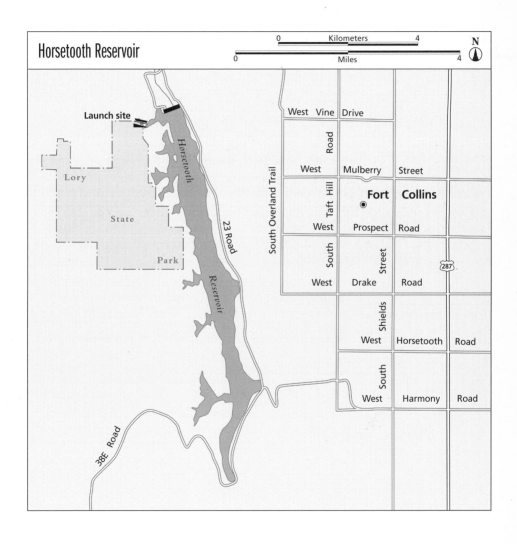

Horsetooth Reservoir

A mother and daughter team enjoys a warm summer afternoon paddling on Horsetooth Reservoir.
COURTESY OF BOULDER OUTDOOR CENTER

28 Boulder Reservoir

Boulder Reservoir offers the active small city of Boulder its only real beach and lake for recreating. Set on the eastern edge of town, Boulder Reservoir is surrounded by small rolling hills set out on the Front Range plains rather than within the mountains. This can be a busy place in the warm summer months, but because no motors are allowed on the lake, it can still feel peaceful.

For the best paddling—and to escape the crowds on the south side beach—head to the western edge of the reservoir and paddle the coastline around to the northern edge of the reservoir. The crowds are left behind, the roads are a bit in the distance, and abundant waterfowl can be encountered in the marsh grasses.

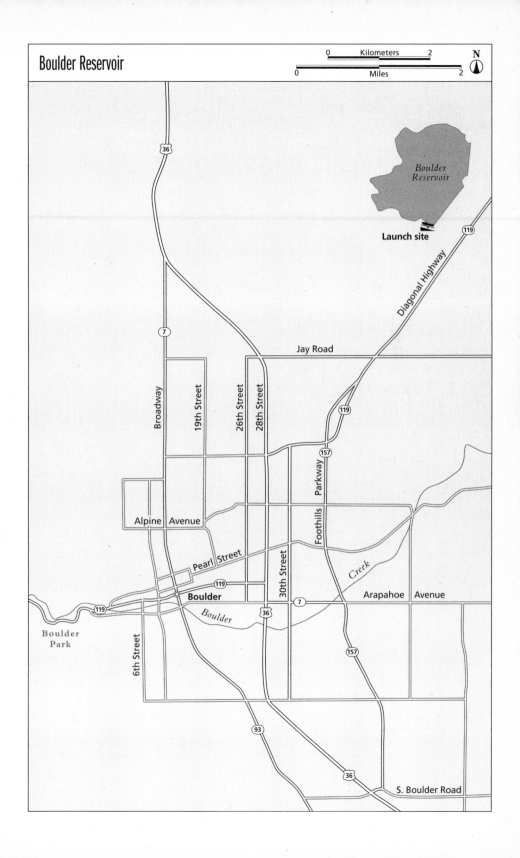

Distance: 1.0 to 5.0 miles (as long as desired)
Launch site: South Beach
Craft: Rec boats, canoes, kayaks
Approximate paddling time: 1 to 3 hours
Season: April through October; year-round possible
Access: From downtown Boulder, head east on Pearl Street out to the Foothills Parkway past 30th Street. Head north on the Foothills Parkway then the Diagonal Highway toward Longmont and look for Jay Road at a traffic light. Turn left (west) onto Jay Road. Shortly thereafter, take your first right (north) onto 51st Street and follow signs for the reservoir. Turn right into the park. Pay the entrance fee and park near the boat ramp on the south side of the reservoir; this is the launch site.

Additional information: For more information on Boulder Reservoir, call (303) 441-3468 or visit www.bouldercolorado.gov.

Honorable mention: Gross Reservoir, west of and above Boulder.

29 Chatfield Reservoir

Chatfield Reservoir offers a 5,300+–acre flatwater oasis in a sea of urban-ness. Because of its proximity to the Denver metro area, Chatfield is a busy, busy place. Avoiding the crowds and motors, flatwater paddlers will find a worthy afternoon tour that will feature a less populated area of the reservoir that is home to more waterfowl and wildlife.

From the launch site, paddle toward the western edge of the reservoir and head up the southern arm. This is the outflow of the now-dammed South Platte River and is also home to a heron rookery. Farther upstream at the mouth of the river, the marshlands also offer a protected cove away from it all.

Distance: 1.0 to 3.0 miles
Launch site: South Ramp
Craft: Rec boats, canoes, kayaks
Approximate paddling time: 1 to 3 hours
Season: May through September
Access: From downtown Denver, head south on Interstate 25 to exit 207B. Veer right (west) onto U.S. Highway 85 (Santa Fe Drive). Continue heading south approximately 7 miles to Highway C-470; enter C-470 turning right and heading west. Get off at the next exit, which is Wadsworth Boulevard. Head south on Wadsworth, eventually crossing over the southern arm of the lake. At a T-intersection turn left (north) onto County Road 5 and follow signs to Chatfield State Park. Pay the entrance fee and follow signs for the South Ramp; this is the launch site.

Additional information: For more information on Chatfield State Park go to http://parks .state.co.us/Parks/Chatfield/.

Honorable mentions: Bear Creek Lake Park, east of Morrison; Cherry Lake, Cherry Creek State Park in Aurora

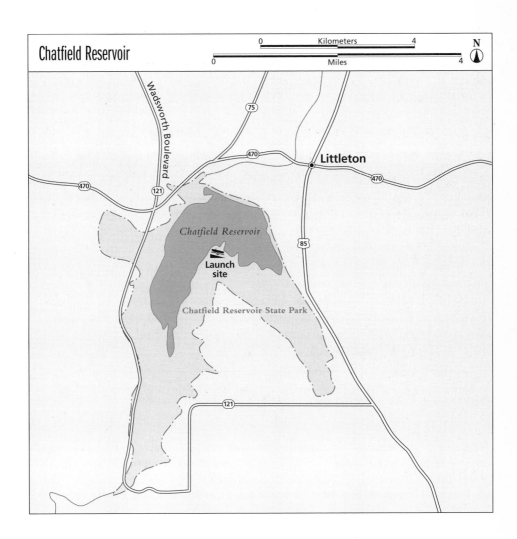

A group of paddlers enjoys an after-work paddle on Chatfield Reservoir.
COURTESY OF RENAISSANCE GUIDES

30 Lake Pueblo

Lake Pueblo State Park is a nice site for an afternoon flatwater tour on the western edge of 4,600+-acre Lake Pueblo. The northwestern end of the lake is more suitable to flatwater paddling, as there are fewer personal watercraft and larger craft in the area.

From the launch site, head across the reservoir to the southern edge and then head west along the coastline, heading upstream. Paddling farther to the west will have you encountering the outflow of the now-dammed Arkansas River. Part of the northern end of the lake is called Swallows. Once a small community that was flooded when the lake was formed, Swallows is home to a large number of birds and is a layover spot for migrating pelicans twice a year. Enjoy this area set beneath the Wet Mountains just to the west.

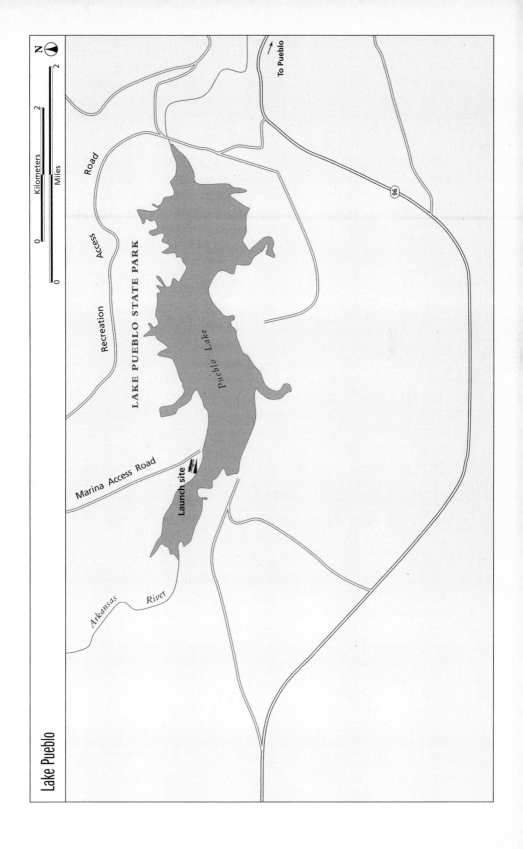

Distance: 1.0 to 6.0 miles
Launch site: Northshore Marina
Craft: Rec boats, canoes, kayaks
Approximate paddling time: 1 to 3 hours
Season: April through October; year-round possible
Access: From downtown Pueblo, head east to Interstate 25; enter the interstate heading north. Get off at exit 101 for U.S. Highway 50 and head west on US 50 toward Pueblo West. Pass Purcell Boulevard. Turn left (south) onto McCulloch Boulevard and follow this down around toward the entrance station at Lake Pueblo State Park. Pay the entrance fee and follow signs for Northshore Marina; this is the launch site.
Additional information: For additional information on Lake Pueblo State Park, visit http://parks.state.co.us/Parks/lakepueblo.
Honorable mention: The small St. Charles Reservoir, south of Pueblo

31 Lake Granby

With 7,250 acres and more than 40 miles of shoreline, Lake Granby is the second-largest body of water in Colorado. Set at the foot of the Continental Divide just outside the western boundary to Rocky Mountain National Park, Lake Granby offers endless miles of flatwater touring with a majestic mountain backdrop. Crowds and motors can be an issue here, but there is room for everyone; and there is a nice, more-isolated tour along the northern edge of the reservoir.

From the launch site, paddle across the reservoir, island hopping along the way. Or take a detour and paddle up the Grand Bay arm of the lake. Stay along the northern edge of Lake Granby for more a more-isolated hillside paddle. Trails closely parallel this side of the reservoir.

Return back across the reservoir, or continue all the way down to the eastern arm of the lake to Arapaho Bay and paddle back along the southern shore.

Distance: 1.0 to 10.0 miles (or as long as desired)
Launch site: Sunset Point, Arapaho National Recreation Area
Craft: Rec boats, canoes, kayaks
Approximate paddling time: 1 to 4 hours
Season: May through October
Access: From Interstate 70 head north on U.S. Highway 40 toward Winter Park. Head up and over Berthoud Pass, drop down into the Fraser River Valley, and continue heading north through Fraser and Granby. Just west of Granby turn right (east) onto U.S. Highway 34 and head east into Arapaho National Recreation Area. Look for signs for Sunset Point; this is the launch site.
Additional information: For additional information on Lake Granby, go to www.grand-county.com/Granby.aspx. For additional information on Arapaho National Recreation Area (Sunset Point), visit www.fs.fed.us/r2/arnf/recreation/anra/index.shtml.
Honorable mentions: The eastern edge of Shadow Mountain Lake, just to the north of Lake Granby; Williams Fork Reservoir, to the west of Lake Granby

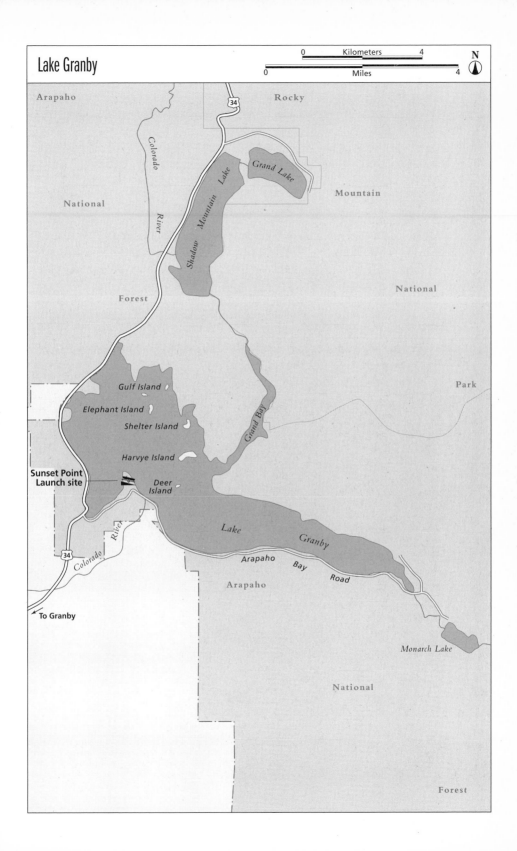

Lake Granby

Kilometers
0   4
0   4
Miles

N

Arapaho   Rocky

34

Colorado

River   Mountain

National

Shadow Mountain Lake

Grand Lake

Forest   National

Park

Gulf Island

Elephant Island

Shelter Island   Grand Bay

Harvye Island

**Sunset Point
Launch site**   Deer
Island

Lake   Granby

34   Colorado   River   Arapaho   Bay   Road

Arapaho

To Granby

Monarch Lake

National

Forest

32 Lake Dillon

Lake Dillon, the largest lake in the area, is set at 9,000+ feet beneath the dramatic Continental Divide, which towers above the eastern edge of the reservoir. The lake was originally created to divert water out of the Blue River Basin into the South Platte River Basin to quench Denver's thirst. Sprawling out at 3,200+ acres with approximately 27 miles of shoreline, Lake Dillon offers flatwater recreation for all types of users—motorboats and sailboats as well as canoes and kayaks.

The most frequently used access is from Dillon Marina on the north side of the lake. For a nice paddle, go along the east edge of the reservoir, heading up the quiet and fish-friendly area within the Snake River Arm. A longer add-on option is to come out of the Snake River Arm and keep heading to the south, checking out the eastern edge of the Blue River Arm. Fir trees line the banks, and trails closely parallel this entire side of the reservoir.

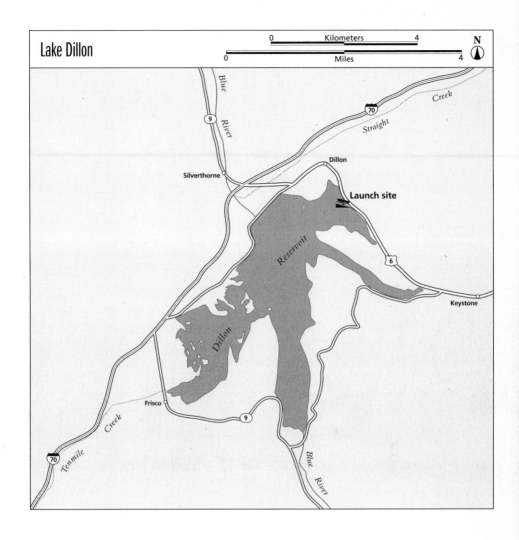

Lake Dillon

A brother and sister team enjoys the waters of Lake Dillon.
COURTESY OF WILDWASSER SPORT

Distance: 1.0 to 8.0 miles

Launch site: Dillon Marina

Craft: Rec boats, canoes, kayaks

Approximate paddling time: 1 to 5 hours

Season: May through September

Access: From downtown Denver, head west on Interstate 70, head through Eisenhower Tunnel (underneath the Continental Divide), and drop down toward Dillon. Take exit 205 (Silverthorne), and then head east for 2 miles on U.S. Highway 6, going underneath the inter-state, toward Dillon. Follow signs for the Dillon Marina; this is the launch site. Another launch site is available at the Frisco Bay Marina, which is accessed off I-70 exit 203.

Additional information: For additional information on Lake Dillon, visit www.townofdillon.com. For information on the launch site, visit www.dillonmarina.com.

Honorable mention: The western edge of Green Mountain Reservoir to the north

33 Blue Mesa Reservoir

At 20 miles long with over 95 miles of shoreline, Blue Mesa Reservoir is the largest body of water in the state. Blue Mesa is set within the Curecanti National Recreation Area and offers numerous designated campsites, picnic areas, launch sites, and trails. Once on the water, countless inlets and coves offer ample paddling exploration options; but along with the miles of exploration come hordes of crowds—mostly with motors.

The reservoir is also well known for its fishing, having broken the state record with a fifty-plus-pound trout pulled out of its waters. Fear not—there are a few quieter coves worthy of exploring that also offer fine kayak fishing.

The Dillon Pinnacles trailhead on the west side of the U.S. Highway 50 bridge is a good launch site that offers a variety of flatwater options. Putting in here, it is possible to stay along the north edge of the reservoir, heading up into the quiet West Elk Arm.

If you're looking for a longer edition on this northern side of the reservoir, paddle back down the West Elk Arm. Instead of returning to the launch site, continue heading west up Soap Creek Arm. This is a busier arm of the reservoir, as there is a boat launch area at the northern end.

For a longer day tour from the same launch site, explore the Lake Fork Arm on the south side of the reservoir. With all this water, there are plenty of options for paddling.

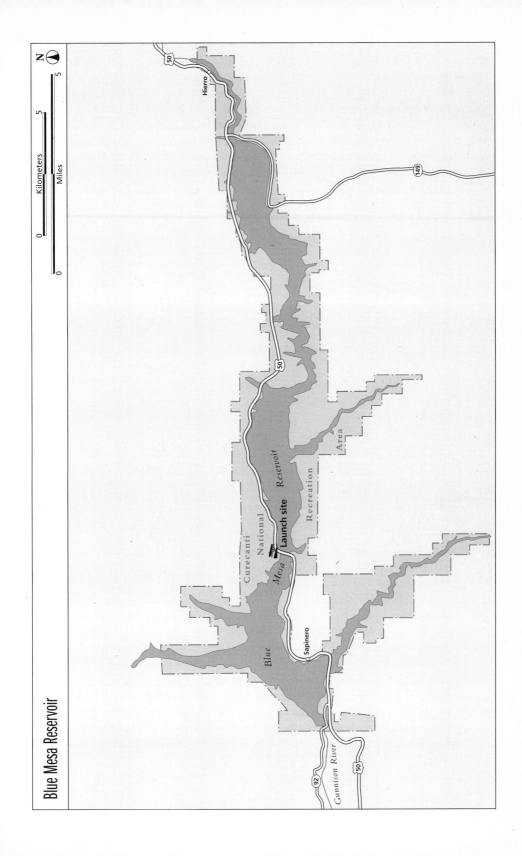

Distance: 1.0 to 20.0 miles (as long as desired)
Launch site: Dillon Pinnacles trailhead
Craft: Rec boats, canoes, kayaks
Approximate paddling time: 1 to 6 hours
Season: May through October
Access: From downtown Gunnison, head west on US 50, paralleling the Gunnison River. The river drops into the backwaters of Blue Mesa Reservoir. Continue on US 50 west. Just before US 50 crosses the reservoir, there is a sign for Dillon Pinnacles Access. Turn right and wind

down toward the reservoir; this is the launch site. Another launch site is available at Sapinero, farther west on US 50, for exploration up the Lake Fork Arm.

Additional information: For additional information on Blue Mesa Reservoir and Curecanti National Recreation Area, visit www.nps.gov/cure. Park headquarters can be reached by calling (970) 641-2337.

Honorable mention: Ridgway Reservoir, within Ridgway State Park, southwest of Blue Mesa

34 Vallecito Reservoir

Vallecito Reservoir is tucked away in the southwest corner of the state. This very nice paddling destination gathers the drainage from the Weminuche Wilderness Area (the largest wilderness area in the state). Set beneath towering mountains less than an hour's drive above the Western-flavored town of Durango, Vallecito is a beautiful flatwater getaway that provides 2,700+ acres of flatwater.

The most common access is to launch on the northern end of the reservoir next to the inflow from Vallecito Creek (this is also a great fishing area). You will find a bit quieter paddle along the northeastern edge of the lake by heading south. Pine and fir trees fall into the steep-sided reservoir as paddlers pass Forest Service picnic/camping areas on their way to the mouth of the Los Pinos River inflow into the reservoir (another good fishing spot).

It is possible to continue paddling down the eastern edge of the reservoir all the way to the dam. Simply reverse course and get a great view of the mountains while returning to the launch site on this fine half-day paddle.

Distance: 1.0 to 6.0 miles
Launch site: North end of lake
Craft: Rec boats, canoes, kayaks
Approximate paddling time: 1 to 4 hours
Season: May through October
Access: From downtown Durango, head east on U.S. Highway 160 to the traffic light in Bayfield; turn left (north) onto County Road 501 (Vallecito Road). Head up the Pine River Valley, eventually passing Vallecito Dam and driving around the western edge of the lake. Stay on CR 501; on the northern side of the lake, the

road turns to dirt. Within 0.5 mile after CR 501 becomes dirt, look for dirt pullouts along the right-hand side of the road next to the lake. These pullouts are launch sites.

Additional information: For additional information on Vallecito Lake, call (970) 247-1573 or visit www.vallecitolakechamber.com.

Honorable mentions: The nice mountain lakes of Haviland and Electra, to the north of Durango; the northern arm of McPhee Reservoir, just north of Cortez

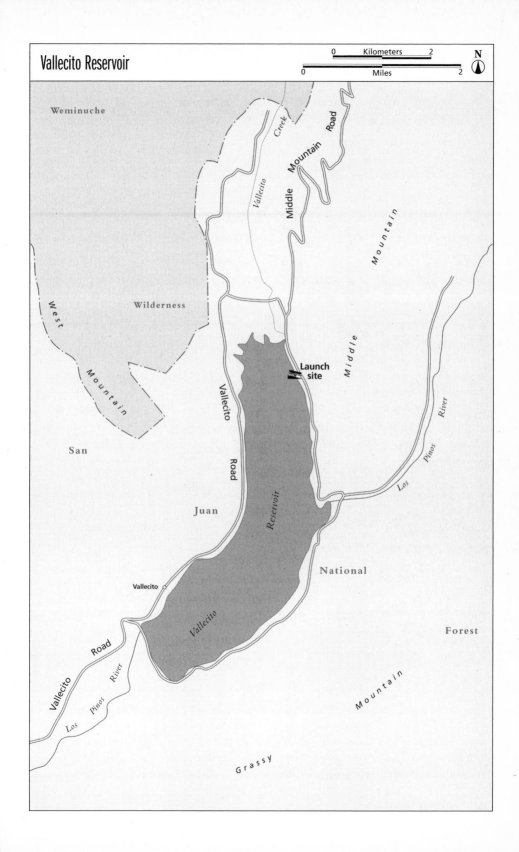

Vallecito Reservoir

0 Kilometers 2
0 Miles 2

N

Weminuche

Vallecito Creek

Middle Mountain Road

Mountain

West

Wilderness

Mountain

Middle

Launch site

Vallecito Road

San

Los Pinos River

Juan

Reservoir

Vallecito

National

Los

Forest

Vallecito Road

Vallecito

Los Pinos River

Mountain

Grassy

Luna barks commands to Brad Higginbotham during an afternoon paddle on Vallecito Reservoir.

Appendix: Paddling Resources

Books

Banks, Gordon, and Eckhardt, Dave. *Colorado Rivers and Creeks* (Boulder, Colorado: 1999); www.kayakingcolorado.com.

DeLorme Maps. *Colorado Atlas & Gazetteer* (Yarmouth, Maine: 2007); www.delorme .com.

Cassady, Jim, Cross, Bill, and Calhoun, Fryar. *Western Whitewater* (North Fork Press: 1994).

Stafford, Evan, and McCuthchen, Kyle. *Whitewater of the Southern Rockies,* (Wolverine Publishing: 2007); www.wolverinepublishing.com.

Web Sites

Eddyflower—National paddling resource Web site
www.eddyflower.com

Mountainbuzz—Colorado's boating forum Web site
www.mountainbuzz.com

Paddling Life—National online paddling magazine
www.paddlinglife.net

Paddling Gear

Adventure Medical Kits—First-aid kits
www.adventuremedicalkits.com

Astral Buoyancy—Personal flotation devices
www.astralbuoyancy.com

Kavu Clothing—Off-river wear
www.kavu.com

Liquidlogic Kayaks—Kayaks
www.liquidlogickayaks.com

Patagonia—Clothing and luggage
www.patagonia.com

Prijon/Wildwasser—Kayaks
www.wildnet.com

Snapdragon Designs—Sprayskirts
www.snapdragondesigns.com

Sweet Helmets—Helmets and head protection
www.sweetprotection.com

Watershed Drybags—Waterproof bags
www.drybags.com

Werner Paddles—Paddles
www.wernerpaddles.com

River Permit Information

Arkansas River
Arkansas River Headwaters Recreation Area
307 West Sackett Avenue
Salida, CO 81201
(719) 539-7289
http://parks.state.co.us/Parks/ArkansasHeadwaters

Green River—Lodore and Whirlpool Canyons
Dinosaur National Monument
4545 U.S. Highway 40
Dinosaur, CO 81610
(970) 374-2468
www.nps.gov/dino/river

Yampa River
Dinosaur National Monument
4545 U.S. Highway 40
Dinosaur, CO 81610
(970) 374-2468
www.nps.gov/dino/river

Miscellaneous Permits and Information

Colorado State Parks
http://parks.state.co.us

River Flow Information

U.S. Geological Survey (USGS)—National Water Information System
http://waterdata.usgs.gov/co/nwis/rt

Watertalk—Colorado Streamflows
(303) 831-7135
www.dnr.state.co.us/water/flow

Flows can also be checked on the following Web sites
www.mountainbuzz.com
www.eddyflower.com

Paddle Shops/Schools/Clubs

Alpenglow Sports
Golden, CO
www.alpenglowco.com

Alpine Quest Sports
Edwards, CO
www.alpinequestsports.com

Alpine Sports Outlet
Boulder, CO
www.alpinesportsoutlet.com

Backdoor Sports
Steamboat Springs, CO
www.backdoorsports.com

Boulder Outdoor Center
Boulder, CO
www.boc123.com

Canoe Colorado
Denver, CO
www.canoecolorado.com

Centennial Canoes
Centennial, CO
www.centennialcanoe.com

Colorado Kayak Supply
Buena Vista, CO
www.coloradokayak.com

Colorado Whitewater Association
Englewood, CO
www.coloradowhitewater.org

Confluence Kayaks
Denver, CO
www.confluencekayaks.com

Durango Whitewater
Durango, CO
www.dgowhitewater.com

The Edge Ski & Paddle
Pueblo, CO
(719) 583-2021

Front Range Paddlers Association
Golden, CO
www.whitewaterracing.org

Four Corners Riversports
Durango, CO
www.riversports.com

Glenwood Kayak
Glenwood Springs, CO
www.glenwoodkayak.com

Pikes Peak Whitewater Club
Colorado Springs, CO
www.pikespeakwhitewaterclub.com

Poudre Paddlers
Fort Collins, CO
www.poudrepaddlers.org

Pueblo Paddlers
Pueblo, CO
www.pueblopaddlers.org

Rocky Mountain Adventures
Fort Collins, CO
www.shoprma.com

Rocky Mountain Canoe Club
Englewood, CO
www.rockymountaincanoeclub.org

Rocky Mountain Sea Kayak Club
Lakewood, CO
www.rmskc.org

Renaissance Guides
Lakewood, CO
www.raguides.com

Three Rivers Resort
Almont, CO
www.3riversresort.com

Colorado River Conservation Organizations

American Whitewater
P.O. Box 1540
Cullowhee, NC 28723
(828) 293-9791
www.americanwhitewater.org

Arkansas River Trust
332 1/2 West Sackett
Salida, CO 81201
(719) 539-0700
www.akrivertrust.org

Colorado Environmental Coalition
1536 Wynkoop Street, #5C
Denver, CO 80202
(303) 534-7066
www.ourcolorado.org

Colorado Whitewater
P.O. Box 4315
Englewood, CO 80155
www.coloradowhitewater.org

Headwaters Institute—Arkansas River
Nathrop, CO
www.headwatersinstitute.org

Sierra Club—Rocky Mountain Chapter
2260 Baseline Road, Suite 105
Boulder, CO 80302
www.sierraclub.org/co

Colorado River Events

Icebreaker Race (late April)
Clear Creek, Golden, CO

PaddleFest (mid-May)
Arkansas River, Buena Vista
www.coloradokayak.com

Gunnison River Festival (late May)
Gunnison River, Gunnison, CO
www.whitewaterpark.org

Lyons Outdoor Games (late May/early June)
St.Vrain River, Lyons, CO
www.lyonsoutdoorgames.com

Mountain Games (late May)
Eagle River, Vail, CO
www.tevamountaingames.com

Animas River Days (early June)
Animas River, Durango, CO
www.riversports.com

Yampa River Festival (mid-June)
Yampa River, Steamboat Springs, CO
www.backdoorsports.com

Fibark (late June)
Arkansas River, Salida, CO
www.fibark.net

Gore Canyon Race (mid-August)
Colorado River, Kremmling, CO

About the Author

Freelance photographer and writer Dunbar Hardy has been focusing on the paddlesports industry for more than fifteen years, with articles and photos published in national and international publications. He has also held the position of senior editor for *Kayak Session* and *Paddle World* magazines.

Dunbar is recognized as one of the most experienced and accomplished expedition paddlers/leaders in the world. He has successfully completed first descents and paddling expeditions throughout Colorado and the United States, as well as in such exotic places as Bhutan, Russia, Morocco, China, Mexico, Honduras, Guatemala, Costa Rica, Panama, Venezuela, Ecuador, Peru, Chile, Argentina, New Zealand, Italy, France, Switzerland, and Canada. He is also a co-owner/lead instructor of Tarkio Kayak Adventures (www.teamtarkio.com), based in Missoula, Montana, which offers domestic and international multi-day instructional kayaking clinics.

After literally traveling the world paddling, Dunbar is proud to call Colorado his home.